JB JOSSEY-BASS

Center for
Creative
Leadership
NORTH AMERICA EUROPE ASIA
www.ccl.org

Building Character

Strengthening the Heart of Good Leadership

Gene Klann

BICENTENNIAL
1807
WILEY
2007
BICENTENNIAL

John Wiley & Sons, Inc.

Published by Jossey-Bass
A Wiley Imprint
989 Market Street, San Francisco, CA 94103-1741   www.josseybass.com

Jossey-Bass books and products are available through most bookstores. To contact Jossey-Bass directly call our Customer Care Department within the U.S. at 800-956-7739, outside the U.S. at 317-572-3986, or fax 317-572-4002.

Jossey-Bass also publishes its books in a variety of electronic formats. Some content that appears in print may not be available in electronic books.

Library of Congress Cataloging-in-Publication Data

Klann, Gene.
    Building character : strengthening the heart of good leadership / by Gene Klann.
        p. cm.—(A joint publication of the Jossey-Bass business & management series and the Center for Creative Leadership)
    Includes bibliographical references and index.
    ISBN-13: 978-0-7879-8151-8 (cloth)
    ISBN-10: 0-7879-8151-6 (cloth)
    1. Leadership—Study and teaching. 2. Character. 3. Integrity. 4. Leadership—Moral and ethical aspects. I. Title.
    HD57.7.K546 2007
    658.4'092—dc22

                                                            2006026719

Printed in the United States of America
FIRST EDITION
HB Printing   10 9 8 7 6 5 4 3 2 1

A Joint Publication of

The Jossey-Bass

Business & Management Series

and

The Center for Creative Leadership

Contents

Preface

Recent news brings us a steady flow of reports on character failures of leaders and influential personalities in corporations, sports, the entertainment industry, politics, religion, and nonprofit organizations. Of course, all humans are flawed by varying degrees of weakness and shortcomings, and character lapse is nothing new in leaders. What is disturbing, however, is the current frequency of failures, the range and depth of their impact, and their span across virtually every type of business and occupation.

This book is for leaders who are concerned about this problem and who understand that the character of their own cadre of leaders affects the productivity, culture, and reputation of their organization. The book is for practicing leaders and managers in corporations, nonprofit organizations, the government, and the military. More specifically, it is for those who may want to address the problem by developing positive leadership character in their subordinate leaders, employees who are being groomed for supervisory positions, employees who show high leadership potential, and other key individual contributors. Inasmuch as all employees have some degree of leadership potential, this book is really about processes that can be used to develop the leadership character of all your employees. The book is also for anyone taking part in such a process.

Leaders have an inherent responsibility to further develop their cadre, including in the area of leadership character. Before doing so, however, it's implicit that the leader must become an outstanding role model for leadership character. The leader must set the example.

This book will give practicing leaders and managers practical tools, information, and processes for further developing their own and others' leadership character. It gives practical ways to establish and ensure sound leadership behaviors.

As I wrote this book, I was keenly aware that there was, as yet, no readily available basic reference or substantial set of guidelines regarding this challenge. Many well-written books address character as a general concept, and some touch on the topic of character for leaders, but none outlines a practical model on how to actually develop leadership character in others. Having led others in the military and elsewhere for more than thirty years, I know how much those of us who recognize the need to develop, rather than just look for, strong character in others need a sound resource. I intend this book to fill that need. A starting point for the book is defining what positive, effective leadership character is—what it looks like, its dynamics, and its potential benefits.

The book is not a discourse on the moral meltdown of the West or the moral collapse of the United States. It will not attempt to evaluate whether the nature of humankind is basically either good or bad. It won't present a monolithic moral code, nor attempt to mandate, prescribe, or direct anyone's behavior. Nor will it address every possible situation. It doesn't pretend to be the definitive work on character, character development, or leadership development.

But it will draw on my experience as a leader and teacher of leaders, and on my work at the Center for Creative Leadership (CCL), which is itself an excellent example of how the culture of an organization can promote positive leadership behaviors that influence institutions and situations much larger than itself. The book *will* provide you with a framework for instituting leadership character development within your organization. It will describe a process based on good fundamentals, best-practice insights, and common sense. This is a practical book. I've tried to make it simple, direct, realistic, practical, and firmly grounded by examples.

Greensboro, North Carolina   GENE KLANN
September 2006

Acknowledgments

First and foremost, I would like to thank my wife, Kathy, who possesses the most sterling leadership character of anyone I have ever known. She was also my able research assistant, sounding board, critic, encourager, and spur! I would also like to thank my children, Kim, James, and Eric, for their support, encouragement, insights, and personal examples of character.

Thanks to my dad, mom, and sisters, Joann and Audrey, who were the key leaders in the development of my own leadership character. Hoping against hope, they always displayed incredible patience and resilience!

I must also recognize several outstanding leaders of character who have been an inspiration to me: Bob and Mary Gunn, Coach Ron Akin, Charles Lange, Colonel Mike Barry, Major John Ernser, Principal Bob Meissner, Professor Michael Boll, Coach Bill Ebert II, Ron Sweetman, Ellen Ramsey, Jerry Hersh, Paula Brown Stafford, Joseph Nelson, and Vincent Manzi.

My sincere appreciation also goes out to those colleagues with whom I discussed this work and who offered comments, suggestions, changes, and criticisms, especially Pete Scisco and Ellen Van Velsor. Thanks also to Felecia Corbett for her invaluable assistance with my research. A special thanks to Alan Venable, whose accomplished editing skills and wide range of insights and talents helped make this book a reality.

About the Author

Gene Klann is a senior member of the training faculty at the Center for Creative Leadership in Greensboro, North Carolina. Prior to joining the Center in 1999, he was founder and president of *Leadership International*, an organization specializing in human relations, training, coaching, and management consulting. During that same period, he conducted training at the Michigan Leadership Development Institute at Saginaw Valley State University, where he designed and delivered a leadership series for key business and community leaders.

Gene retired from the U.S. Army in 1994 after twenty-five years of distinguished service. His career included service in Vietnam, Germany, Panama, the first Gulf War, and Italy, and culminated with service at the U.S. military delegation to NATO headquarters in Brussels. He successfully completed five tours as a unit commander. Gene was awarded seventeen personal military decorations, including three for valor and fourteen for specific acts of achievement or meritorious service.

Gene earned his B.A. in history from Ripon College, his M.A. in international relations from the University of Arkansas, European Campus, and his Ph.D. in philosophy from the Free University of Brussels. He also received a diploma as a U.S. Army War College fellow from the NATO Defense College in Rome.

His first book, *Crisis Leadership*, was released in 2003. His second, *Building Your Team's Morale, Pride, and Spirit*, was released in 2004.

As the personal highlight of his career, Gene takes special pride in having commanded a battalion of six hundred paratroopers in Desert Shield and Desert Storm, and seeing that all six hundred returned to the United States alive.

Chapter One

Character and Leadership

Who was the best leader you ever worked for?

Why?

Who was the worst?

Again, why?

Take a moment to answer.

As you thought about the first two questions, you probably thought of some good leader you have known and mentally assigned words and concepts like *competent, trustworthy, positive, dependable, cared about people,* or *kept us informed.* The memory of a bad leader probably summoned a list of opposites: *incompetent* (or *only marginally capable*), *pessimistic, didn't care about anyone else, wouldn't share information.*

For both leaders, you probably remember specific behaviors that you thought were good or bad, and the behaviors probably followed a pattern. Over time, for better or worse, most leaders exhibit consistent patterns of leadership behavior. The pattern shapes their reputation (how they are known and perceived by others), is considered a reflection of their character, and largely determines their standing and status with others.

Leader behaviors that are considered positive and constructive can be attractive and highly influential. The result is greater respect and trust, and stronger emotional connection between such leaders and their employees. These are behaviors that leaders should strive to develop in themselves, in the cadre of leaders below them, and in all their employees.

The word *develop* raises several questions: Can good leadership be developed, especially insofar as character is concerned? Can an adult's character be deliberately improved? If so, what attributes of character are most important to focus on in developing better leadership? Finally, are there specific approaches and methods that an organization can pursue?

The answer to all these questions is yes. The aim of this book is to help you, a practicing leader, to further build and develop leadership character in your organization's leadership cadre as well as in yourself. The book will look at leadership character first and foremost in terms of behavioral patterns that have a positive, consistent, and useful influence on others. Later chapters will lay out a systematic framework for organizing your efforts. They will also provide a number of tools and suggest specific effective methods.

For now, let's consider a bit more why these efforts are needed, what it really means to lead, and how a focus on behavior makes character development possible.

What's Currently Missing from Leadership Development

While we all agree that leadership is important, we also seem to agree that there is a problem with the performance of our leaders. The results of a joint survey by Harvard and *US News and World Report* regarding leaders in the United States confirms this. Of the 1,374 people polled, 73 percent responded that most leaders in the United States are out of touch with the average person, 58 percent felt their leaders cannot be trusted, only 39 percent felt they have high ethical standards, and only 28 percent said they are the best Americans can do ("Poll: A Leadership Deficit," 2005). Nearly 60 percent of those polled believe the country would be better off with more women in leadership positions. Military and medical leaders got the highest leadership marks, and leaders of the press got the lowest. From this survey one can reasonably conclude that there is a leadership deficit in the United States. Considering the daily international news, it is not unfair to say that there are varying degrees of leadership shortfalls around the world and in many fields of endeavor.

In the course of my own interviews with many leaders in business and other organizations, I have found that while they and their organizations pay a good deal of lip service to the subject of leadership character, they do very little of substance about it. What is done? For example, new employees, including leaders, are briefed by human resources on corporate values and standards of behavior (but after that they hear nothing). A list of company values is commonly posted somewhere in a frame (but never emphasized or discussed). Posters from publishers like Successories focus on character, integrity, and related principles (but hang unnoticed in common areas). There may also be some innocuous rating item regarding integrity on the performance appraisal form—or a course about ethical dilemmas offered by the corporate online training university (but very rarely anything with real teeth or substance).

Beyond that, character development work has traditionally been limited to defining appropriate and inappropriate behaviors in areas such as sexual harassment, diversity and affirmative action, sensitivity training, and employee standards of conduct. Even in organizations that are more advanced, character development has not gone much beyond group discussion on how to handle situations posing ethical dilemmas. The task of defining and instilling moral and ethical attitudes or behaviors seldom gets more than a passing look.

How can these behaviors be defined? What needs to be instilled?

First, let's draw an important distinction between managing and leading. Although many people know there's a difference, in practice the two are often confused. But management deals with such tasks as planning, designing, directing, controlling, coordinating, and tracking execution. By contrast, leadership is about motivating, inspiring, encouraging, and influencing people. We lead people and manage things. Real leaders are effective at leveraging and shaping reality with intangibles such as vision, hope, spirit, morale, emotion, enthusiasm, passion, and soul. Good leaders have positive influencing attributes like courage, caring, self-control, optimism, and communication skills. Good management matters, but it is much easier to find or train good managers and administrators than it is to find or train good leaders. Of course, some nominal leaders have only slight impact and influence because, in fact, what they primarily do is manage. But what they miss—and what is hard to find—is a genuine people orientation and the special relational skills that a really effective leader must have.

Leadership has the potential to become your organization's most valuable resource. Everything new that happens or does not happen in your organization—including any response to change—depends on the quality of your leaders. The success or failure of a company's vision, products, programs, systems, and processes all depend on leaders' setting the atmosphere, tone, and example for the entire organization. Exceptional leadership can have a strong, positive multiplying effect. This is particularly true of the organization's senior leaders, but it is not limited to them. For better or worse and more or less, leaders on every level will affect their sphere of influence.

Really good leadership is a rare and precious commodity—increasingly so as organizations face new complexities and challenges at the global level. The good news is that you don't need to mine the depths of the earth for great leaders. You can develop the leaders you have.

To Lead Is to Influence

Basketball Hall of Fame coach John Wooden said that a life not lived for others is not a life, and that there is no greater joy than doing something for others (Wooden, 1997). Rick Warren begins his best-selling book *The Purpose Driven Life* with the words, "It's not about you" (Warren, 2002).

These ideas go directly to the heart of what it means to lead. Being a leader of character means that life is not so much about what you yourself can accomplish as it is about caring for and behaving so as to meet the needs of others in ways that bring out their best. To lead is to influence. An effective leader possesses the skills and abilities to influence others for the best—prompting, stimulating, motivating, persuading, dissuading, convincing, and encouraging. An effective leader is always thinking, "What impact does my behavior have on others?" "What might others think, feel, or do as a result of what I do?" "Is my behavior effective, ineffective, or neither?" "How can I behave differently to be more influential?"

Of course, a leader's influence can be positive or negative. Adolf Hitler, Joseph Stalin, and Saddam Hussein possessed the ability to influence, but their ultimate influence was basically self-serving and obviously negative. Others, such as Gandhi, Mother Teresa, and Florence Nightingale, also possessed the capacity to influence but used it more positively, focusing on the needs of others and not on themselves.

Effective and positive influence does not usually flow out of simply applying official authority, title, position, or regulations. Often an authoritarian approach is ineffective in motivating others to do what is needed. Effective leaders must develop skills in a range of other more positive ways to influence. In *Leadership in Organizations* (1989), Gary Yukl lists numerous tactics commonly used to persuade or convince others, among them ingratiating, exchanging (quid pro quo), building coalitions, making inspirational or personal appeals, consulting, legitimizing, and pressuring. Yukl suggests that managers can categorize these tactics as being either positive or negative. For example, pressuring and micromanaging to achieve results (such as frequently checking on a direct report's progress on a specific assignment) will generally have negative consequences. On the other hand, personal appeals based on a legitimate relationship between leaders and their leadership cadre (founded not just on title or position but also on common interests and values) can achieve significant results.

In the past, leaders were expected to influence their direct reports. Today, however, leaders are also expected to influence their superiors, board members, peers, customers, clients, suppliers, the news media, community officials, political leaders, government regulators, negotiators, environmental authorities, special interest groups, Wall Street analysts, and any number of other stakeholders. To meet these demands of leadership, rank is clearly not enough, and each group requires different tactics to be influenced and led both effectively and positively. Leaders need flexibility and many different skills to communicate credibly and interact with all these parties for maximum results. The principles found in this book address the kinds of influence that extend in all directions.

The idea of leadership as influence also points to a difference between a focus on effectiveness and a focus on *success*. The difference is not just semantic. Of course, leaders should be successful, but a better gauge is whether they are truly effective in terms of influence. Leaders can be considered successful when they achieve the goals and objectives for which they are responsible—that is, when they "make their numbers." But suppose that in the course of making those numbers, half the workforce leaves the organization and morale of those remaining is low. Or suppose much greater success was possible if everyone in the organization had really taken part? True effectiveness means using leadership influence to unite the organization's efforts toward and past any single bottom-line moment. It means achieving goals and objectives in such a way that the team is still intact, morale is high, and people are lined up to get on the team.

By these criteria, General H. Norman Schwarzkopf, commander of the victorious coalition forces in the first Gulf War, is an excellent example of an effective leader. His victory was one of historic proportion and he did it with less than three hundred U.S. deaths—very literally keeping the team intact. Even one soldier's death is one too many, but in contrast it was estimated there would be approximately ten thousand U.S. deaths in that conflict.

Focusing on Behaviors

Traditionally character has been defined as "the combination of emotional, intellectual, and moral qualities that distinguishes a person." It derives from the Greek *kharassein*—to engrave, inscribe, or sketch. In other words, character means qualities that are internally engraved in people, becoming an integral part of them. These qualities are then reflected in a person's pattern of behavior. Thus, leaders' behavior reflects what they stand for and what their core nature is.

Different people see leadership character attributes as more or less fundamental to character behaviors. Frances Hesselbein, founding president of the Drucker Foundation, defines leadership as a matter of how "to be" as a leader and not how to do or say something (Adrian, 2001). On the other hand, when it comes to leading, certainly what we *do* in the literal sense outweighs whatever we merely say or profess to be true. As Ralph Waldo Emerson wrote in *Letters and Social Aims,* we don't have to say very much because what we do "thunders" so loudly that no one hears a word we are saying.

Leadership character is all about behaviors. A leader's behaviors are a combination of attributes: traits, qualities, and skills. Leadership character is defined as behaviors that have a positive influence on others. It is how leaders behave (based on what inner qualities they may possess or thoughts they may cherish) that determines their reputation and good name.

Leadership behaviors refer mainly to conduct in the presence of others: actions, comments, nonverbal signals, and personal mannerisms, as well as general demeanor, deportment, and comportment. Like anyone else, leaders can behave badly or they can conduct themselves properly and suitably. Leaders can display positive and constructive behaviors or those that are negative and destructive. Whichever they display, their behaviors will be understood as a reflection of who they are.

I mentioned early that leaders are viewed according to their overall patterns of behavior. For the greatest leadership influence and impact, consistency matters. Consistency extends beyond the idea of "rising to the occasion." Leadership character is not just seen in leaders' behaviors related to crisis, in the presence of stress, or in situations involving an ethical dilemma; it shows up in all behaviors and in everything they do or fail to do. This is crucial point, because we tend to talk in terms of how a leader handled a certain crisis or made a difficult or potentially controversial decision, but what is equally important (or more so) is how the leader consistently and positively communicates, solves problems, makes decisions, resolves conflicts, disciplines others, builds teams, or casts a vision from day to day. Daily and common behaviors tell much more about the character of a leader than the periodic tough decisions do or the way the leader handles the single great crisis of a career.

For leaders, consistency means always reflecting the same basic principles in practice. It means that one's behaviors conform and agree with one's past words and actions regardless of pressure, criticism, and advice to do otherwise. It means maintaining the habitual positive behaviors that are key to winning trust and respect and achieving effectiveness overall. It means being seen and known as a pillar of dependability and reliability, not changing or wavering based on opinion polls, internal disapprovals, or external condemnations.

Consistency also implies that a leader's behaviors and character are not compartmentalized between work and personal life. You are who you are, and that doesn't change when you arrive at the office or at your own front door. Your character is such that you find consistent standards for behavior in any context. Responsibilities, stresses, and personalities may vary, but your character does not. All the politically correct arguments to the contrary do not change that reality. Behaviors reflect a leader's character regardless of the context. In every context, your character will be noticed and judged.

Leadership Character Can Be Developed

The Greek philosopher Heraclitus said, "A man's character is his fate." There is truth in this fatalistic view. Every person's character is founded on early experiences and influences in childhood and adolescence. These come from home life, schooling, interactions with peers, part-time or summer jobs, and spiritual institutions. They're provided by role models such as parents, grandparents, older siblings, teachers, coaches, spiritual leaders, and by society in general.

Such contacts and exposures largely determine people's patterns of behavior, their value systems, personal moral codes and creeds, convictions, principles, and beliefs. In these forms, a person's character accumulates over time.

But Heraclitus' view does not rule out character *development*—the idea that character can change through an ongoing, continual process of growth, maturation, and improvement. Leadership character involves for the most part learned behaviors, which can be observed and assessed by others. If you learn how to conduct yourself in a certain manner, your behavior will reflect a certain quality such as courage, caring, self-control, optimism, and ready communication. None of these attributes is innate and all five of them lie at the heart of effective leadership.

You can develop the behaviors that define leadership character both in yourself and in others. A person may have a natural inclination or a genetic predisposition to behave in a certain way. Psychologist Carl Jung's "type theory" advanced the idea that we are all hardwired toward certain behavioral preferences. But Jung also believed that we can and do learn to behave contrary to our preferences (Jung, 1976).

All the behaviors involved in leadership character are ones that can be learned by adults regardless of age. As humans, we never lose the ability to learn. This is not to say that changing behaviors is always easy. A behavior that a person has practiced for several decades will not change overnight. However, a rational, emotionally healthy, and psychologically stable person of any age can see an advantage to changing certain behaviors and act upon that perception.

A basic thesis of many religions, such as Judaism, Christianity, and Buddhism, is that people can change their behavior to become more moral and virtuous. These religions contain moral codes and numerous writings on how to do this and apply the principles of their teachings. It is well documented that many people have made dramatic behavioral changes after having a major religious experience.

For centuries the military, through intense discipline and aggressive training, has taken civilians and prepared them to function on the battlefield. That transition is probably the most dramatic change of behavior possible. It is done routinely and in most every country with varying degrees of success.

The key, as I implied earlier, is to go about change in terms of adjusting behavior. Jean Piaget was among the first psychologists whose work focused on character development. He believed that all development evolved from action; people create their understanding of the world though their interactions with their surroundings (Piaget, 1965). He believed that through this process character, too, was developed. Although he worked primarily with children, his theory applies to adults just as well. Through the results of and feedback from their behaviors, through reason and reflection, people can determine which behaviors are appropriate and effective and which are inappropriate and ineffective. Through this process of personal discovery and problem solving, they can then adjust their future behaviors.

My own experience is that adults change their behavior to gain something positive or to avoid something negative. In the first instance, what they stand to gain looks more important to them than preserving an old behavior. For example, people reduce how much they eat because of how good they expect to look and feel after losing weight. Regarding the second instance (avoiding a negative consequence), in a former role as an executive coach, I had clients sent to me who were told by their employer that if they did not respond to my coaching and change their behaviors they would be terminated. It was amazing how motivated these coachees were to avoid that negative consequence.

Adjustment (as opposed to wholesale, instant change) is really the key word in developing better leadership behaviors. The development process helps leaders make adjustments to current behaviors that will lead to greater influence and effectiveness. The process begins with understanding about the impact of current behavior that comes from feedback, personal reflection and introspection, and other sources. Once leaders understand the impact of their leadership behaviors, either positive or negative, they can choose to change how they behave.

Constructive and Affirming Behaviors

Having defined leadership character in terms of behaviors that have a positive influence on others, I need to say more precisely what behaviors are truly constructive and affirming, highly influential, and ideally universal. Later chapters go into more detail, but for now here is a useful overview.

First are the behaviors implied in what is known as the "Golden Rule": *Do unto others as you would have them do unto you.* The Golden Rule is essentially universal, inasmuch as it is found in all the major religions in the world. It tells us to use the same behaviors toward others as we would want them to use toward us. At a minimum this means treating others with respect, dignity, and equality, being sensitive to their needs and emotions, listening to them, paying attention to them, and so on. As an exercise, try listing your own specific desires for how you want to be treated by others. Then think about how that list might serve in guiding your own behaviors as a leader.

Less well known is the "Silver Rule." The Silver Rule says that we should *not* treat others the way we would *not* want to be treated. Whereas the Golden Rule is active, the Silver Rule is restrictive—not using behaviors on others that we do not want to be used on us. For example, most of us don't want to be

- Told a lie
- Deceived by false or incomplete information
- Injured by someone's self-focused, thoughtless, rude, or insensitive behavior
- The subject of a negative rumor or gossip
- The victim of sexual innuendo, harassment, or assault
- Defrauded out of money, property, or goods
- Called stupid, ignorant, uneducated, or ugly
- Discriminated against because of race, religion, gender, or ethnic background
- Treated with disrespect, unwarranted distrust, or in an undignified manner

Many times when discussing patterns of behavior, the Silver Rule provides a clearer perspective and understanding than the Golden Rule. We know how frustrated and angry being treated in these ways can make us. We also know what we would think of someone who consistently did so.

Yet another perspective is provided by the "Law of Reciprocity," which says that the way *you* behave toward and treat others is the way they are likely to behave toward and treat *you*. Leaders who be-have in an unseemly manner open themselves to this law.

It is really in everyone's best interests to behave according to the Golden and Silver Rules in attitude, speech, and conduct. But it is also possible to go beyond them in the search for universally ac-knowledged positive and negative attributes of leaders. In 1993, The Wharton School of Management at the University of Pennsylvania began a global study on leadership and organizations (House et al., 2004). The researchers interviewed 17,500 middle managers in sixty-two countries and eight hundred organizations. Among other interesting findings, there emerged a list of fifteen leader attributes or descriptions universally acknowledged as positive: communicative, informed, courageously decisive, positive (optimistic), trustworthy, honest, just, dependable, team builder, motivator, encourager, dynamic, intelligent, a win-win problem solver, and planner. For leaders exploring which attributes to focus on for leadership behav-ior development, this list is a good place to start. (Later in this chapter I boil it down to a smaller, more manageable set.) There were also seven universally acknowledged *negative* attributes for leaders: loner, asocial, irritable, dictatorial, ruthless, noncoopera-tive, and egocentric.

Many of the constructive and affirming leadership behaviors on the list may strike you as intuitive, much like the Golden and Sil-ver Rules—and perhaps they are. But in most situations they are still very useful. However, sometimes leaders face dilemmas that re-quire other orders of thinking. For example, leaders may need to choose behaviors based on ideas of the greater good, the lesser evil, reconciliation of competing values, or consistency with their own and the organization's broader systems of values. These challenges require thinking of behaviors not just in terms of rules but also in terms of personal values that underlie behaviors.

Values, Needs, and Behavior

Public opinion and the majority viewpoint are seldom good starting points for making decisions and choosing behaviors. History shows that the majority view has often been totally wrong. Vivid examples in U.S. history include the support for slavery prior to the Civil War, racial segregation for the hundred years after the Civil War ended, and the denial of women's right to vote as late as 1920.

Developing positive leadership behaviors requires some more independent concept of what drives individuals' behaviors in the first place. It is generally accepted that each of us has two broad types of drives: our values and our needs. Values generate needs, so I'll start with the former. In essence, values are those things that really matter to us, including our essential beliefs, attitudes, principles, and priorities.

How do people acquire values? Building on the work of Piaget, developmental psychologist Lawrence Kohlberg proposed a theory of the development of moral reasoning and character. He saw the process as made up of six stages that an individual could achieve only in sequence, beginning in early childhood with relatively simple concepts of obedience and punishment and ranging up to an advanced stage of behavior based on values and independent conscience that most adults never actually reach. In Kohlberg's view each stage of moral reasoning represents a significant shift in the behavioral perspective of the individual, and the goal of character development is to help individuals build on experience to advance as far as possible in sequence upward through the stages.

Kohlberg's theory reinforces the concept of character and moral development as an ongoing, lifelong process. Other theorists have seen this development as a process in which, throughout our lives, our moral perceptions and values are formed and reshaped by various experiences, communications, rules, laws, conventions, moral teachings, rewards, recognitions, punishments, and so on (Simon, Howe, & Kirschenbaum, 1995).

Every day, consciously or unconsciously, we base choices, decisions, and actions on our personal system of values. Everything we say or do (including our habits) reflects that system. But some elements of a personal system of values are more enduring and central than others. On one hand we possess core values that seldom change. These values are often related to family and other close relationships, health, security, and so on. On the other hand, we hold more transitory values that are important for the moment but change. These values may be related to the circumstances of a current job, place of residence, hobby, recreational activity, and so on.

Leaders need to be as aware as possible of their own values. With awareness, we can see how well we integrate and manifest those values in our daily life. A useful tool for this purpose is "values clarification," a process that is well described in *Values Clarification: A Practical, Action-Directed Workbook* (Simon, Howe, & Kirschenbaum, 1995). It outlines seventy-six strategies for helping leaders understand their personal values system, ranging from "Rogerian Listening" to an exercise called "What's in Your Wallet?"

Appendix A of this book is another resource—a brief assessment instrument for helping you clarify your personal value system. It can help you to identify what may be hidden or unconscious values, as well as help you notice where your values conflict with one another.

As noted, our values generate our needs, which brings us closer to actual behaviors. For example, if one of my core values is the welfare of my family, then I will have a need to spend time with them, support them, and ensure their safety and security. Determined by my values, these needs will then drive much of my behavior.

Two fundamental theories can greatly assist us in understanding our own needs. First is the work on human needs by psychologist Abraham Maslow. In 1943, he published the first edition of his core research on the topic (Maslow, 1987). He proposed a five-level hierarchy of human needs. He believed that as we meet the needs at one level we automatically go on to have the needs of our next level met.

According to Maslow, the foundational level includes physiological needs such as food, water, air, sleep, and sex. The second level up includes needs related to safety and security—protection, stability, and consistency. The third level brings in our social needs, such as being part of something larger than ourselves and receiving validation and social acceptance from others. The fourth level is the need for respect and esteem from others. The fifth—top—level is a need for "self-actualization," which means reaching our full potential and becoming all that we are capable of being.

Will Schutz provides more perspective on interpersonal needs. According to Schutz's model, we all have three interpersonal needs: inclusion, control, and affection. Inclusion has to do with relationships and associations; it determines the amount of contact a person seeks. Control has to do with our need to be in charge, to have influence, and to bring order and structure to a situation. Affection has to do with our need for warmth in relationships, open and honest communication; it determines the closeness we seek with others. Schutz provides a means of assessing how much of each interpersonal need you express to others (what others see in your behaviors) and how much you desire from other people in each of the three areas of interpersonal need. Schutz developed a personality assessment to help individuals become aware of their own interpersonal needs. Called the Fundamental Interpersonal Relations Orientation— Behavior, it is generally known by its acronym, FIRO-B (Schutz, 1958, 1996). The booklet has fifty-four questions. It can be of great assistance to leaders in understanding how their needs drive their behaviors.

But keep in mind that personal values systems have limits. Leaders of character know that under no circumstances should their pattern of leadership behavior, decision making, or efforts to influence be based on their own individual desires or whims. No individual has that degree of authority. The idea that every person can make this determination can only lead to confusion, contention, and anarchy. Defining what are positive or negative behaviors isn't a matter of any one person's individual preferences but a combination of things including established laws; custom and tradition; cultural norms; social acceptability; personal values; organizational values and standards; spiritual beliefs; common sense, logic, reason, moderation, and balance; and the norms of honorable conduct. In other words, personal values are only one of ten items to be considered when defining leadership character.

Choices, Consequences, and Dilemmas

Approaching the end of this introduction, I want to underscore the importance of choice. The Greek philosopher Aristotle advocated an early form of the scientific method—that one should investigate the natural laws and facts of the world. From this experience, assisted by reason, Aristotle maintained that a person can then come to know the absolute truths of the universe, and from there go on to live in an ethical manner and thereby achieve *eudaimonia*, or happiness (*Internet Encyclopedia of Philosophy*, 2006). In other words, Aristotle saw living a life of virtue as the perfection of reason, and ultimately a matter of choice. The life of virtue depended on consciously choosing behaviors in line with twelve virtues, among which Aristotle included courage, sincerity, modesty, temperance, and liberality. He believed that to achieve happiness, one needed to choose behaviors representing a balance among the virtues.

Every day as a leader you face choices, alternatives, options. At a critical moment in the movie *Precinct 13*, a character says that the most powerful thing in life is the ability to choose. I agree. So does award-winning actress Meryl Streep, who says that we are the result of the choices we have made over our lifetime.

In every situation we face, we can choose how to respond and what to do or not do. Because our choices matter so much, *how we go about making choices* is a key part of leadership character development. One general guideline is that our choices should be consistent with one another, our value system, and our organization's value system. That often means reviewing a range of options, trade-offs, and alternatives, considering the consequences and impact of each, and choosing among them.

Beyond that, good decision making also means maturely owning and taking full responsibility and accountability for the choice. Good leadership character means being answerable and liable for choices and whatever other behaviors a leader commits. It involves the old-fashioned concept of being responsible and accountable for everything the organization does or doesn't do. That includes taking the credit for the decision and its results, whether it yields accolades or criticism.

When making major choices, leaders often face problems on every side. They may well have no clearly right choice, only sets of needs and disadvantages to balance against one another. Arguments can be made for and against every option in such a situation, leaving leaders with a number of alternatives, all of which may be filled with ambiguity. Arguments can be made on both sides of a dilemma. In such situations, leaders have a number of alternatives, all of which may be filled with ambiguity. For instance, one choice may conform with societal, cultural, or organizational values and standards of behavior, another may not, and a third may be open to interpretation. There may be a choice that will require choosing between increasing profits at the expense of the employees. Then there is the dilemma that arises when a leader's personal values collide with the organization's values. Sometimes the best choice may be among a group of options that are all weak. Because such dilemmas pose many problems, I will pay special attention to them later in the book.

In short, this book relies on your choice. It does not presume to deliver a program in support of any particular system of values or beliefs beyond the basically universal concepts of positive leadership behavior mentioned earlier in this chapter. The book does address general and best-practice leadership behaviors; it suggests and recommends; but again, it's up to you to choose behaviors according to your own frame of reference.

As a leader in your organization, it's also in some large part up to you to choose whether or not your organization can benefit from an active program of leadership character development. Only someone who is really providing leadership and not simply filling a leadership position will consider creating a character development process for the rest of the cadre of leaders. Developing people and helping them meet their full potential is a leader's—not a manager's—role.

The Five E's: A Framework for Character Development

The second chapter of this book explores a set of attributes that go a long way to clearly define the leadership behaviors that you and your organization probably want to develop. The five chapters after that lay out a framework for developing leadership character in an organizational context. I call the framework the "Five E's" (Klann, 2003a): *example, experience, education, environment,* and *evaluation.* As you will see, the Five E's approach makes intuitive sense. If you'd already stopped and asked yourself, "How can I build a program for developing character in my organization's leaders?" you might well have come up with a framework like this.

Example

Example refers to a leader's influence on others through their observation of the leader's behaviors. It is the most powerful way to develop character because it leverages the natural human tendency to emulate the behavior of individuals who are respected, held in high esteem, or in positions of authority. Within any organization the behaviors of these leaders set the standard for everyone else.

Experience

Experience refers to developing leadership character by exposing leaders to new and challenging leadership work. This can include a variety of assignments, such as serving on a task force or special project, moving to positions with increased or different responsibilities and scope, heading a start-up or fix-it, or shifting from operations (line) to staff or vice versa. Experience also includes activities like attending a highly experiential leadership development training course—for example, the Center for Creative Leadership's globally renowned organizational simulation, The Looking Glass Experience. Experience also refers to the developmental possibilities of hardship or failure.

Education

Education refers to providing knowledge and training to a leader related to leadership character development. Organizations can set up formal and informal training that focuses on relevant behaviors and how they demonstrate character, the potential pressures on and challenges to character resulting from such things as performance expectations and market competition, and the short- and long-term implications of a lapse of character. Education might include discussions of dilemmas and scenarios that involve difficult moral or ethical choices.

Environment

Environment is essentially the organizational culture and its values system, both formal and informal, in which a developing leader functions. An organization's environment plays a huge role in either encouraging or impeding the character development of leaders. You can shape your organization's culture to support and promote constructive leadership behaviors.

Evaluation

There are many ways to apply the feedback, performance appraisal process, and disciplinary practices of an organization to develop leadership character. In their own behavior, people will generally pay closest attention to things for which they know they are being held accountable. Leaders will pay close attention to these areas of behavior that are being rated in the ongoing course of performance appraisals and decisions regarding merit increases, bonuses, and promotions. This accountability can play a key role in the process of developing leadership character.

Each of the "Five E's" chapters emphasizes practical, how-to leadership character development. The final chapter provides more guidance for planning and initiating an overall program of character development for leaders.

Building Leadership Character: Getting Started

1. What in your own view is missing from leadership character today, in general or in your organization?

2. In what ways do you currently see yourself and your cadre of leaders as being effective and influential? In what ways not?

3. In your own experience, can you recall a situation in which you could see that a leader's character went through some improvement, either as part of some deliberate training or in some other setting? (Think in terms of improved or adjusted behaviors.)

4. How well does the Golden Rule serve as a model for how to treat others? Make a list of ways that you want to be treated by others. Could that list also serve as a cornerstone for your own leadership behaviors? Try again, using the Silver Rule.

5. In what ways do the "Five E's" make general sense to you as a complete range of approaches to developing leadership character among your own cadre of leaders?

Chapter Two

Five Influential Attributes

As I said in Chapter One, leadership character is behavior that has a positive influence on others. Behaviors reflect underlying attributes—personal characteristics, traits, qualities, and skills that can be ascribed to the person. A leader's attributes can have a positive influence on others, which is good, or they can have a negative influence, which is bad.

This chapter describes five attributes that are remarkably influential in leaders in all organizational sectors—public, private, or nonprofit:

Courage

Caring

Optimism

Self-control

Communication

Although there are others I could discuss, these five attributes are particularly central to the Five E's in the next five chapters. Leaders who develop their professional leadership behaviors based on these attributes will appreciably increase their overall influence, effectiveness, and productivity as leaders.

Attributes must be inferred from behavior. For example, if I see a leader such as Mother Teresa who behaves with compassion and empathy, I would assign her the attribute of caring. If the leader's behavior reflects daring, nerve, and risk taking, as in the case of

General George S. Patton Jr. during the Battle of the Bulge, then he would be assigned the attribute of courage. Similarly, Marianne Moore, the American poet and modernist writer who won virtually every major American literary award, including the Pulitzer Prize and the National Book Award, also behaved in ways that indicate courage, along with other traits such as patience and loyalty (Joicey, 2002).

Each of the five attributes relates to behaviors that involve making choices, as John McCain points out in *Character Is Destiny* (2005). In turn, the choices lead to consequences for which a leader of character must take responsibility.

Let's consider each attribute by itself, then discuss briefly how they interact.

Courage

There are two kinds of courage: physical, and moral or managerial. Physical courage usually involves a single act, such as running into a burning building or jumping into a raging river to save a life, or acts of bravery like those that individuals such as Medal of Honor winners Sergeant Alvin York in World War I and Lieutenant Audie Murphy in World War II displayed on a battlefield. Many Americans remember the example of Ronald Paul Bucca, a New York City fire marshal who died in World Trade Center Tower Two while attempting to rescue workers and evacuate the building. He was known as the "Flying Fireman" because he had fallen from the fifth floor (and survived) during a previous rescue attempt in a burning building. Britons know of Constable Deborah Russell-Fenwick, who was decorated by Queen Elizabeth II for her heroic efforts during the London terror bombing attack of July 7, 2005.

However, the type of courage that needs to be developed for leadership character is moral courage or managerial courage. Moral courage means standing up for one's convictions and values while risking criticism, censure, ridicule, or persecution. It can also mean a willingness to risk loss of power, position, possessions, or reputation. It means doing what you believe is right and being willing to take an unpopular position regardless of external or internal pressures not to. It also means believing that the consequences, whatever they may be, are less important than the position you are taking.

Compared with physical courage, moral courage is far more rare, perhaps by a ratio of ten to one. True, an act of bravery can threaten both life and limb. At the same time, it tends to involve a situation that has a distinct beginning and fairly immediate end. This is one main reason that behaviors involving physical courage are generally easier for most people than those of moral courage. An act of moral courage is not life threatening, but it may have long-term and potentially very negative consequences, including loss of job, reputation, and future opportunities.

Moral courage involves taking risks and accepting the fear that goes with potentially losing something very important to present or future security. Yet what will be gained from the act of moral courage will generally not be for self but for the benefit of another individual, the team, the organization, the community, or society in general.

The attribute of moral courage is revealed when leaders stand up for direct reports who have made a mistake or are being criticized by others, tell the truth even if there could be very negative consequences, challenge unethical decisions, question ill-conceived and self-serving or impossible tasks, share unpopular or contrary opinions, make controversial or divisive decisions, or point out areas that could potentially cause embarrassment to the organization.

In his Pulitzer Prize–winning book, *Profiles in Courage* (1956), John F. Kennedy tells the stories of eight U.S. political leaders who were faced with difficult situations and decisions that required a high degree of moral courage. Two are especially noteworthy.

The first is the story of Edmund G. Ross, the freshman Republican Senator from Kansas who in 1868 cast the decisive vote against his party's position on the impeachment trial of President Andrew Johnson, in spite of enormous pressure and criticism. Had

Ross voted with his party, President Johnson would have been re-moved from office. Ross based his decision on the principle that the integrity and separate powers of the three branches of federal gov-ernment should be preserved. He believed that if the Senate re-moved the president, the executive branch would be weakened and subordinated to the will of the legislative branch, which he consid-ered bad for the long-term political health of the country. As a re-sult of his vote, Ross was branded by the press (in the sensational language of the time) as a Judas Iscariot and a Benedict Arnold. His fellow Republicans and many of his former supporters in Kansas treated him like a pariah. His image was burned in effigy. He was not elected to a second Senate term and died in poverty and dis-grace. Ross was keenly aware of his personal stakes at the time he cast his vote. He said that making the decision on how to vote was like looking down into his own open grave. However, Ross was will-ing and able to look beyond his immediate personal fortunes and see the greater long-term consequences of his choice: his decision preserved the intent of the Founding Fathers regarding the respon-sibilities and relationship of the government's three branches. The positive impact of Senator Ross's morally courageous decision re-mains with all Americans today.

Another of Kennedy's subjects, Sam Houston, was nationally recognized as a hero for his leadership in a victory over a Mexican army commanded by General Santa Anna at San Jacinto in 1836. Much earlier in life, in 1814, he had been seriously wounded in a battle with Native American Creek and Cherokee while serving under Andrew Jackson's command at Horseshoe Bend, Alabama. Dating back to that experience, Houston regarded Jackson as a mentor and always remembered Jackson's maxim that a man with courage makes a majority.

In the course of his career, Houston was also selected as the first president of the independent republic of Texas, was elected to both houses of Congress, and was governor of both Tennessee and Texas. However, despite being governor of Texas, Houston was opposed to any Southern state seceding from the Union. He believed that secession was constitutionally wrong and that the tension between the northern and southern states over slavery needed to be worked out instead by debate and compromise. He also believed that secession would only lead to a war that could not be won by the secessionist states.

As the American Civil War was beginning in 1861, at the age of sixty-eight, Houston traveled all over Texas outlining his ideas on the issue. As a result he was branded a coward and a traitor to the Southern cause. He faced ugly mobs, insults, stones, and even the dynamiting of the hotel in Waco where he was staying. When the Texas legislature voted to secede from the Union, Houston sadly resigned from his post as governor. As it turned out, everything he had prophesied about the consequences of the decision to secede from the Union came true, including much loss of life and property in the Civil War. Thus taking a courageous stand does not always have the desired result, but leaders of character make the courageous choice and anticipate success. As an old proverb has it, "Nothing great or even good happens without courage."

In the opinion of Winston Churchill, "Courage is the first of all human qualities because it guarantees all others." As Claire Booth Luce, writer, congresswoman, and diplomat, put it, courage is the ladder on which all other virtues mount (Munier, 2004).

President John F. Kennedy agreed, noting that everyone admires courage, and the greatest garlands go to those who possess it. It was the leadership attribute he admired most. In fact, the key characteristic of those he would select for government positions was that they had a demonstrated record of courage. He believed that such a person could always be counted on.

The Positive Influence of Courage

Like physical courage in battle, a single morally courageous moment can earn a leader instant and lasting respect. More than two centuries ago, when British admiral Horatio Nelson praised U.S. commodore Stephen Decatur's attack on Tripoli Harbor in the Barbary pirate conflict as the most bold and daring act of the age, Decatur's name became legend (Axelrod, 2003). Conversely, a leader can also forever lose respect by failing to behave courageously when the situation calls for it.

What accounts for this great influence of courage? One reason that showing managerial courage inspires respect is that it is often recognized as being, by and large, a selfless form of behavior. Routinely, human nature is fundamentally self-focused. People will normally do what's in their own best interests. They go along with the crowd, do what's safe and conventional, or, as Fox News analyst Bill O'Reilly says, "They hide under their desk."

By the same token, people are rightly impressed when someone makes a sacrifice for others, particularly if they themselves benefit from the sacrifice.

Another reason that courage heightens esteem is that we recognize courageous behavior as a sign of having overcome fear. Like other people, almost every leader struggles with at least one sort of fear—of failure, public speaking, embarrassment, or displeasing others. These fears cause many people to play it safe, seek comfort, and place their security above their values. But as Mohandas Gandhi said, cowards can never be moral (P. Anderson, 1992). More ominously, Dante claimed that the hottest places in hell are reserved for those who, in a time of moral crisis, maintain their neutrality!

Courage is not the absence of fear but carrying on in spite of fear. It has such a great influencing value because the majority will take the easy road and only a small minority will take the brave one. Knowing this, people trust, honor, and revere the courageous. Pope John Paul II was held in high esteem because of, among other things, his moral stand against communism and all other forms of repressive government.

Courage yields respect also because it implies that leaders take responsibility for their own actions. Responsibility means being answerable for the discharge of a duty or trust. A courageous leader, and that leader alone, will give account for a group and the results it achieves. If things do not go well the leader of character will say, "Yes, I accept full responsibility for what happened."

Unfortunately this type of behavior is becoming more and more rare. A more common approach is to shift responsibility and blame someone or something else.

The leadership philosophy and principles of Roger Ailes, chairman and CEO of Fox News Channel, are based on responsibility (Hayden, 2005b). Ailes' advice?

- Take responsibility and make decisions.
- Always encourage employees, joke with them.
- Make sure work is fun.
- Tell them the truth and stay open to ideas and feedback.
- Take responsibility if you screw up and change bad decisions as quickly as possible.

This philosophy and its associated behaviors may in part explain Chairman Ailes' great leadership success.

The positive influence of courage also derives from its most frequently moral nature. Lord Moran, a surgeon in the British Army during World War I and also Winston Churchill's personal physician during World War II, wrote about the psychological effects of war in *Anatomy of Courage*, concluding that courage is essentially a moral quality (Moran, [1945] 1987). A moral person would consistently resolve to choose a behavior that feels right. According to Moran it generally comes down to a cold choice between several alternatives. These could include taking action or not, carrying on or quitting, telling the truth or not, and so on. Moran believed that a courageous person's value system causes the choice of right action regardless of the consequences. A coward shrinks into the shadows while the man or woman of courage rises up and does or says what is necessary. Consider Paul Rusesabagina, the Rwandan hotel manager who did not run away or ignore the genocide going on around him in Rwanda in 1994. Although not described as particularly idealistic, at his own risk he bravely sheltered more than one thousand Tutsi men, women, and children simply because he felt it was the right thing to do. For his courage, he received international acclaim and was awarded the highest U.S. civilian award, the Medal of Freedom, at the White House in 2005.

Courage also enhances a leader's decision-making power. (See Appendix B for character-related questions to ask while making decisions.) Leaders with courage are not afraid to make the tough decisions. They do not continually ask for more information. They are able to keep from letting circumstances make them rash, overly cautious, or disorganized. They make decisions in a timely manner and do not avoid the controversial or complex issues. These are additional behaviors that will increase the respect of a leader's cadre.

Finally, courage influences because it is the basis of unusual achievement and progress. It takes courage to pursue a new, controversial, or undeveloped vision or idea. This is the foundation of all progress. Many leaders have new and exciting ideas. They have a vision that could greatly advance society. Granted, some visions may be fantasy—neither practical nor realistic. Other visions are attainable but the leader lacks the courage to make them a reality. A leader of character has the vision, the courage, and the drive to do so. Such people will ignore the fact that their vision may expose them to ridicule, scorn, and laughter. Such people's behavior will make an impact and have a positive influence. Prior to the 1970s the phrase "man on the moon" suggested something crazy and out of reach. President John F. Kennedy's courageous vision of a decade earlier gradually turned that age-old phrase into a common fact.

Caring

Caring means sincere interest in and genuine concern for others. Leaders do not lead in a vacuum; they lead other people. Leadership automatically implies a human relationship. Therefore, leaders with a strong social aptitude, relational skills, and a "people" orientation have a distinct advantage when it comes to influence.

The concept of caring subsumes ideas like consideration, compassion, empathy, sympathy, nurturing, and altruism, as well as love and affection. Unfortunately the last two words carry some meanings that have a negative connotation in the politically correct workplace. In its broad positive connotation, *love* means developing and cultivating strong, healthy, and respect-based relationships. In this context it has nothing to do with physical sex or sexual orientation.

Lorne A. Adrian (2001) asked 150 influential people to name the most important thing they had learned in their life. Thirty-five responded "love." Those doing so included personalities such as Helen Thomas, White House reporter, Bernard S. Siegel, medical doctor and author, Sargent Shriver, president of Special Olympics International, Jeff Getty, AIDS activist, Nobel Prize winners Ilya Prigogine, Torsten Wiesel, and Frederick Willem de Klerk, along with many others.

Sargent Shriver suggested that nothing surpasses the benefits received by a human being who makes compassion and love the objective of life; it is by compassion and love that anyone successfully fulfills life's journey. Yolanda King, oldest child of Martin Luther King Jr., suggested that to love and to be loved are the greatest gift you can give and the most awesome blessing you can receive. Kathleen Kennedy Townsend, former lieutenant governor of Maryland, summed it up when she said, "The most important thing I know is that you must love those you want to lead."

Caring does not mean tolerating or ignoring shoddy performance, violations of company policies, bad attitudes, dishonesty, or slothfulness. Creating a caring culture or environment also does not mean running a business like a country club where people do as they please. It *does* mean seeing humans as the most important resource in an organization—and the one with the most overall potential.

The Positive Influence of Caring

As mentioned in Chapter One, Maslow (1987) posited a hierarchy of five levels of human need. He believed that having our needs met at one level opens the way to being able to have our needs met also on the next, "higher" level up.

Maslow's foundational level includes physiological needs such as food, water, air, sleep, and so on. The second level of needs includes safety and security, reflecting our desire for protection, stability, and consistency.

Our third level of needs is social. Maslow divided this level into two parts: first is the need to belong to something larger than ourselves from which we can gain identity. This need is why people are fans of certain sports teams or performers, join clubs and gangs, or wear hats, shirts, and jackets with an organization's logo. The second social need is the need for receiving acceptance, caring, and affection.

My own experience suggests to me that Maslow's third, social level of need is really the primary human need. In my view, the caring an individual receives is the foundation of a personal sense of security. By their very nature, humans want to be treated with respect, trust, dignity, and equality. They want to be appreciated, validated, and accepted. My experience, including living in seven countries on four continents, has been that this desire is universal.

During my service in the Vietnam and Gulf Wars, I saw soldiers give up, at least temporarily, physiological needs for sleep, shelter, and food to accomplish the mission they were assigned. I also saw them relinquish their need for safety and security and willingly risk their lives to retain their status in and acceptance of their team. So great was this social need to be affirmed and validated that they risked life and limb to have it met.

The principle here is simple yet profound. If leaders treat their followers with caring behaviors such as appreciation, understanding, courtesy, attention, loyalty, and encouragement, the leaders will be rewarded with cooperative and supportive behavior in return.

Characteristically, a leader offering affirmation and validation will get a positive response from the person being affirmed and validated. The recipient will generally offer more cooperation, support, loyalty, and productivity to the leader. Recipients will respect the leader and will work hard not to let that leader down or do anything that might make them "look bad" to the leader. Not only will there be a positive emotional connection between the leader and the led, but validated followers will normally identify with their validating source. Continually, they will turn to it to meet their social needs, so deepening their loyalty to the leader and the team. There will also be a greater sense of commitment and alignment to the group's vision and mission. This will ultimately result in greater efficiency, output, and fulfillment of potential.

A number of very successful and effective leaders add their support regarding the value of caring leadership. Dick Parsons, chairman and CEO of Time Warner, lives by a rule that whatever you sow, you will also reap—the Law of Reciprocity (Parsons, 2005). He received this counsel from his grandmother and believes it was the best advice he has ever been given. He adds, "If I think of anything on a daily basis, in terms of moral compass, that is the one. You treat people the way you want to be treated. If you treat everyone with respect, somehow it comes back to you. If you are honest and aboveboard, somehow it comes back to you."

David Neelman, the founder, chairman, and CEO of JetBlue, tells a story about the impact of his grandfather's caring behaviors (Neelman, 2005). Years ago, Neelman's grandfather ran a general store. If a customer needed something that wasn't currently in stock, he would do whatever was necessary to get the item. At times that meant going down the street to buy the item himself from his competition rather than asking the customer to take the business elsewhere. Neelman says that his granddad never told him, "'Take care of others and they will inevitably take care of you'—he didn't have to. I saw it happen."

Optimism

French emperor and general Napoleon Bonaparte said that leaders are dealers in hope. Optimism is the tendency to take the most hopeful and cheerful view of things and to expect the best outcome. It is having the disposition to look on the bright side of whatever circumstances one is facing. It's being upbeat, positive, and seeing the glass as being half full rather than half empty. Being optimistic is the opposite of being negative, pessimistic, downbeat, cynical, or skeptical. Optimism means absence of despair, despondency, discouragement, gloom, and hopelessness. Optimists seek opportunities, possibilities, and silver linings in every situation. They maintain a sense of hope and confidence about the current situation and the future.

The news media in a democracy have a special challenge with the concept of optimism. Juan Williams, a senior correspondent with National Public Radio, says that to do their job well, the media must be provocative and critical; for example, challenging government decisions and looking for their weaknesses, highlighting reasons plans may not work, and constantly second-guessing. Leaders outside the media—in the private sector, the nonprofit segment, and the majority political party—are not as encumbered by this need. However, even in the private and nonprofit sectors, optimism cannot mean a Pollyannaish attitude that ignores the reality of the situation and lives in denial of the real world. Optimism does require fully accepting reality—but still contending that with hard work, focus, resilience, and a bit of luck, a positive outcome is possible. Interestingly, many clichés about optimism ("Never give up," "All's well that ends well," "When life hands you lemons . . . ") deal with the fact that life is hard and that, to survive, one *needs* to be optimistic. This is especially true for a leader who wants to influence others.

Behaviors associated with optimism include risk taking, innovation, creativity, hopefulness, cheerfulness, good spirits, confidence, buoyancy, and brightness.

Optimism has a psychological magic that can make life seem easier, better, and more hopeful. But can it be learned, or is it simply ingrained in some individuals from early childhood and permanently lacking in others? William James, medical doctor, psychologist, and philosopher, said that the greatest discovery of his generation was that human beings can alter their lives by altering their attitudes. He firmly believed that everyone could change the outer aspects of their lives by changing the inner attitudes of their minds. Recent cognitive and behavioral research by Martin Seligman (1998), past president of the American Psychological Association, supports James's view, describing specific techniques that leaders can use to enhance their optimistic powers.

The Positive Influence of Optimism

How does optimism have positive influence? Like some of the other key attributes, optimism creates a significant emotional connection between the leader and those being led. This is a connection that leaders who grouch will generally not experience. People are naturally drawn to leaders who are positive, upbeat, and cheerful. When something important needs to get done, those being led are motivated and even inspired by a leader who behaves in a way that means "we can do this!"

Optimism also encourages perseverance and patience. When everything looks hopeless, optimism can cause the leader and those being led to keep pushing and driving and not give up. "We will overcome" was the mantra of Martin Luther King Jr. and the anthem of his movement. He had a vision of greater freedom, equality, and equal rights in America. He never gave up, lost focus, or was deterred by what appeared to be slow progress or setbacks.

King's example also demonstrates the important link between optimism and conveying a vision. Optimism causes the leader to step out and take risks on the assumption that what formerly seemed impossible can in fact be done. As Robert Kennedy said, "Some men see things as they are and say why. I dream of things that never were and say why not?"

American Richard H. Truly was a space pioneer who rebuilt the space shuttle program after the *Challenger* disaster. While doing this he lived by the optimistic words of Johann Goethe, who said, "Whatever you do or dream you can, begin it. Boldness has genius, power and magic in it. Try something; start something" (Adrian, 2001).

Optimism is most influential when it is thoroughly ingrained. In professional football, Green Bay Packers coach Vince Lombardi was first and foremost an optimist. He would constantly tell his players that they never lost a game; they just ran out of time. During the Lombardi era, Tom Landry coached the Packers' archrival, the Dallas Cowboys. Lombardi and Landry had been assistant coaches together with the New York Giants. Landry said that when the Cowboys played the Packers and the game was close in the final quarter, he knew that the Packers had a distinct advantage. That was because of the optimism, discipline, and "never say die" attitude that Lombardi had instilled in his team. Leader optimism is influential because it can make your cadre feel like winners and can also intimidate opponents.

Chairman of the U.S. Joint Chiefs of Staff and later Secretary of State, Colin Powell concurs with this basic idea that perpetual optimism is a "force multiplier," increasing an organization's abilities to get the job done and accomplish the mission.

As General Powell notes, an optimistic, can-do attitude pervades much of the U.S. military (Duffy, 2005). Its outlook is that it can accomplish any mission, any place, and any time. I personally benefited from this mind-set when I was selected to command a battalion of paratroopers (the "Nighthawks") in 1989. At the time, the unit had an awful reputation as being hapless and ineffective. When I told one officer at Fort Bragg I'd been placed in command, he responded by asking who I had alienated to get assigned to that loser outfit.

I knew that there are no bad army battalions and that it is the quality of leadership that differentiates good units from bad. With my optimism leading the way, I set up an aggressive program of training, equipment maintenance, caring initiatives, and morale builders to enhance the battalion's pride and overall performance. The total success of this was evident during the unit's subsequent nine-month deployment to the Middle East during operations Desert Shield and Desert Storm. First and foremost, all unit members returned safely to the United States. In addition, the unit had extraordinary mission success. The army recognized this by awarding the Nighthawk battalion the Meritorious Unit Commendation for outstanding performance. Today, when I am asked how I am doing or how things are going, I think back on the multiplying power of optimism and respond, "It's all good." It always gets a smile and other positive reactions.

When asked what is the most important thing he knows, Henry C. Lee, a highly skilled forensic pathologist and a key witness in the O.J. Simpson trial, responded with a code that also reflects the fundamental power of an optimistic outlook (Adrian, 2001):

- The winner is always part of the answer; the loser is always part of the problem.
- The winner always has a program; the loser always has an excuse.
- The winner says let me do it; the loser says it's not my job.
- The winner says it may be difficult, but it's possible; the loser says it may be possible, but it's too difficult.
- Be a winner.

Finally, keep in mind that humor enhances the influence of optimism. Optimistic leaders often use appropriate humor to both motivate and endear themselves to others. In 1981, President Ronald Reagan was shot in an assassination attempt. In the hospital, as he was being wheeled into the operating room with his life hanging in the balance, he was still able to smile and joke with the doctors and staff, saying, "Please tell me that you are all Republicans!" Reagan's positive nature in this very difficult situation enhanced his image and influence at home and abroad.

Self-Control

Self-control means control over one's own emotions, actions, desires, and passions. It is the act, habit, or power of having your energies, faculties, and desires under the control of your will. This includes personal discipline in behaviors and lifestyle. For leaders, self-control also means doing things that normally have a high positive influence on others and avoiding those that in the main have a negative influence. Margaret Thatcher, the first female prime minister of a Western European nation, said that disciplining yourself to do what you know is important and right, although difficult, is the high road to pride, self-esteem, and personal satisfaction (Munier, 2004). Leaders must choose what they will do and not do and then accept the consequences of their choices.

Self-control includes behaving in consistent ways: the leader maintains the same general demeanor whether things are going well or not so well. Self-control also means an ability to be adaptable and flexible when situations change. Shifting circumstances do not agitate the self-controlled leader and cause any overreactions, responses of anger, or visible anxiety.

Self-control implies that you as a leader have sufficient drive and initiative, as well as a clear vision and focus, to concentrate on success-oriented, career-enhancing behaviors. It also requires that your personal behaviors enhance, rather than undermine, your stature. In that regard, here are some basic considerations:

- Physical exercise and physical conditioning
- Weight control; moderate and healthy eating and drinking
- Management of personal finances
- Stress management
- Management of thought and appropriate expression
- Self-education, reading, and personal study

Leadership is very demanding. It requires a great deal of energy, resilience, and stamina. Self-control implies taking care of yourself both mentally and physically. Being in good physical condition will not only enhance your confidence but will also increase your endurance and mental agility. If your basic habits and health are good, aging can be a minor impediment to leadership, even at the highest levels. Not taking care of yourself at *any* age exposes you to potential physical or emotional meltdown.

Self-control includes mastery over personal appetites. It also frees you from the damage, tragedies, and hurts of losing control. Some behaviors can cause considerable personal embarrassment. Even a moment of indiscretion can destroy a reputation and a lifetime of work. If the boss is doing it, that gives the green light for other employees to do it, even if it represents questionable ethics or even violates rules. If indiscretions are part of your consistent pattern of behavior, the only people they will impress and encourage are those who are behaving the same way. Indiscretions involve choices and consequences. You must choose for yourself. Here are some basic behaviors to avoid (there may be others):

- Overindulgence in alcohol
- Use of illegal drugs
- Excessive use of prescription drugs
- Extramarital affairs
- Sexual harassment
- Excessive debt
- Gambling
- Overeating and being overweight

On a flight to Singapore in 2005, a much-traveled European salesman asked his seatmate, Pastor David Crabtree of Greensboro, North Carolina, if he didn't think he missed out on a lot because of his conservative lifestyle? Crabtree responded that yes he did miss out on a lot. He missed out on divorce, ruining his children's lives, causing unwanted pregnancies, getting AIDS or other social diseases, alcohol and drug rehab clinics, psychological counseling, guilt, shame, embarrassment, pangs of conscience, and so on. That response caused the salesman to be very contemplative for the rest of the flight.

Leaders in the public and private sectors might benefit from emulating the work discipline of a number of outstanding and highly regarded athletes. At the age of thirteen, Peggy Fleming, the 1968 Olympic gold medalist and five-time national skating champion, practiced at the local rink from 4:45 A.M. until 7 A.M. Olympic heroine Wilma Rudolph was the twentieth of twenty-two children. When she contracted polio at the age of four, the doctors said she would never walk again. Through hard work and a focused determination, Rudolph made herself walk with leg braces until she could graduate to a special, high-top shoe. She ultimately got rid of the shoe as well and went into competitive sports in school. Through continued hard work and concentration, an indomitable spirit, and grit, Rudolph won three gold medals in running events in the 1960 Olympics.

Cycling legend Lance Armstrong, the only person to win the grueling, two-thousand-mile Tour de France seven consecutive times, said his secret to success is simple: "I always worked harder than the other guy. I would ride when no one else would ride, sometimes not even my teammates." He was taught by his mother never to quit (Armstrong, 2000). This gave him the positive attitude and also the perseverance to beat testicular cancer at the age of twenty-five and subsequently do the impossible by winning the seven Tour de France races. These three athletes epitomize leaders whose inspirational example of self-discipline is a pattern of behavior for all developing leaders to model (O'Neil, 2004b).

As these examples suggest, the difference between unsuccessful and successful people is not a lack of strength or knowledge but a lack of will. As Al McGuire, who coached Marquette University to the NCAA basketball championship in 1977, said, everyone wants to be a great basketball player but few have the work ethic to become that great player. The same principle applies to great leadership. It takes determination, dedication, and focus.

The Positive Influence of Self-Control

For leaders, the influential value of self-control stems first from the fact that self-control is, as just mentioned, a foundation of sustained success, and sustained success, in turn, gives the leader an overall stature and influence.

Self-control is the foundation of long-term personal achievement. It keeps a person motivated and focused on goals. It also contributes to momentum. Without personal discipline, things don't get done. Thomas Friedman's success as a columnist (and author of the best-selling book *The World Is Flat*) has much to do with the fact that he would rise every morning to write from 5 A.M. until 8 A.M. (Brophy, 2005). Then he would do nine holes of golf before going to his office.

The issue is one of fulfilling your personal potential. All leaders may have the desire to be successful and do great things within their range of achievement, but lack of self-control is a primary reason many leaders do not succeed. Potential is never fulfilled in a moment; it's only reached with consistent, continuous effort, which relies on self-control.

When self-control is in place, a leader has the strength of will to do many of the things that others may find extremely difficult, which earns the leader respect and admiration, and ultimately maximal influence.

Similarly, when leaders are able to avoid the temptations and enticements to which they are exposed in leadership roles, this raises their stock with those in their orbit of influence. To avoid temptations, the well-known evangelist Billy Graham always traveled with a male companion as an accountability partner. This person was to keep an eye on Graham to ensure he did not get himself into a compromising situation or do something in which there was even a hint of impropriety.

Although we may not tend to look at things from this perspective until late in life, it should be mentioned that self-control can enhance and ensure a leader's ultimate, long-term legacy. Conversely, leaders whose life was shadowed by a lack of self-control that may not have been obvious to outsiders at the time can suffer significant loss of reputation long after they pass on. For example, the fact that Chairman Mao Tse-tung had one of the world's largest collections of pornography or that President John F. Kennedy had a number of extramarital liaisons did not enhance either of their reputations after their deaths; nor has General (and later President) Dwight Eisenhower's questionable emotional attachment to his British driver Kay Summersby during World War II.

Communication

By the attribute *communication* I mean attitudes and skills that underlie effective direct interpersonal interaction. More basically, communication is simply the transmission of meaning between a sender and a receiver. Notice the primary emphasis on *meaning,* as opposed to simply data, information, or feelings. There are, of course, several methods of interpersonal communication—written, verbal, and nonverbal signs, attitudes, and body language, as well as communication through actions and appearance. Listening is important, too. The communicative leader can take advantage of all these for a positive influence on others.

If it's fair to say that real estate has just three laws ("location, location, location"), I would argue that leadership also has three basic laws: communication, communication, communication. Is it really that important? Winston Churchill said that communication is the difference between mere management and leadership. Anthony Robbins, the well-known motivational speaker, believes that the way we communicate with others and ourselves determines the quality of our lives. Gerald R. Ford, the thirty-eighth president of the United States, gave this piece of advice (Ford, 1979): "If I went back to college again, I'd concentrate on two areas: Learning to write and to speak before an audience. Nothing in life is more important than the ability to communicate."

It isn't always easy to know when communication is happening. George Bernard Shaw captured the unique difficulty of this attribute when he said that the biggest problem in communication is the illusion that it has taken place (Hargie & Tourish, 2004). Every one of us sends out meaning from a certain frame of reference or worldview, and those on the receiving end filter the attempted message through their own, often different, frame and worldview. The endless possibilities for confusion and misunderstanding make it critical to recognize that because instructions or information was "communicated" doesn't necessarily mean it was understood. Many times nothing could be further from the truth. As key principles of effective communication, therefore, at a minimum, a good leader always uses the simplest language, repeats the message, and checks for understanding.

I routinely ask my executive education classes what they think is the principal cause of divorce in the United States. Invariably they suggest financial problems, sexual problems, spouses' outgrowing one another, changing life or career goals, and so on. I then ask what is the core problem behind each of these? At least one person always sees right away that the core issue is communication. One way or another, all these other issues are simply by-products and consequences of poor interpersonal communication.

Communicating Information

In addition to communicating meaning, communicating information is a separate important consideration. Communicated information is the oil and grease that helps an organization operate smoothly. Your cadre and your employees in general need information to do their jobs effectively. More important, they need information to be emotionally connected to the organization. Information increases understanding, confidence, and respect. It makes the recipient feel part of the team—an important part of the organization—and aware of what is going on. Feeling informed can create a positive sense of intimacy within the organization. Not receiving information will feed junior leader and employee insecurities. This will inevitably result in the practice of MSU (Making Stuff Up). The problem with MSU is that what your subordinates and employees make up will inevitably be worse than reality, no matter how bad that reality is! This can all be avoided if you as a leader pay faithful attention to sharing and distributing information.

Roger Ailes, chairman and CEO of Fox News Channel, believes that keeping information flowing is a crucial part of his leadership success (Hayden, 2005b). His philosophy is that the more open the operation, the better. His personal style of operation includes appearing at a podium in the newsroom every quarter to bring people up to date, reinforce the vision and values of the organization, and answer questions for as long as employees have them to ask. He is convinced his cadre and the employees feel more connected to the group enterprise as a result of his open approach. He also gets good ideas from their input. He says:

> I am always surprised when leaders don't do that. When I was down in the pits I used to assume the suits were sitting up there all the time trying to figure out some way to screw me. And that's a natural reaction if you are cut off from management. The problem with many leaders is that they are not open to dialogue with their staff. A leader who does not fear making a decision naturally has no fear of openness. I might make a counter call, because I am relying on my own experience, or because there are factors they don't know about, but I'll listen to everybody and then I'll say no, let's do it this way, and I'll take the consequences for that. [Hayden, 2005b, p. 58]

Listening

Listening is a key element of communication. It is defined as making a conscious effort to be closely attentive, to pay attention, and to focus on what is being communicated. The motivational speaker Zig Ziglar says people are able to speak at 500 words per minute (with gusts up to 650) but can listen at 1,500 words per minute. That disparity means your mind will get bored and begin to drift if you do not concentrate on what is being said. That is also why listening is a skill. We can all hear, but listening requires us to really concentrate on what is being said. It is something that everyone must work on and develop in order to do it well.

When I owned and operated a training business in Michigan, I assisted a number of organizations that were having problems with their unions. Union members invariably would say that management didn't listen to them seriously or intend to respond in a meaningful way. There is a direct relationship between how well listened-to people feel and how much caring they will perceive in the person with whom they're trying to communicate. Good mutual listening fosters a sense of mutual caring. Of course, this is a challenge when one party does not find the other completely credible, doesn't think they know what they are talking about, or sees them as whining, complaining, or repeating things they've said before. Many married couples do not listen to each other in the manner they could because they know (or think they know) intuitively what the other will say and simply don't want to hear it again. But genuine listening is essential. To paraphrase psychologist-pundit Joyce Brothers, listening—not imitation—is the highest form of flattery.

Good listening attitudes and skills confer a great advantage in difficult situations. For example, when Donna Shalala (now president of Miami University) was the new chancellor of the University of Wisconsin-Madison, her first meeting with student government leaders was crashed by Black Student Union leaders, who were angry about the tiny proportion of minority students and faculty, as well as by offensive behaviors from some campus fraternity members (Clark, 2005). Shalala's listening skills, calmness, and promise to do something about real problems defused the entire situation.

Bill Drayton, CEO of Ashoka, is also known as an extremely effective listener (Hayden, 2005a). Ashoka is a global nonprofit organization that aims to find change-making leaders around the world and provide them with support including modest "social venture capital." By this approach, they find that they can transform problematic ingrained institutions and improve lives exponentially. Drayton is seen as a charismatic leader because of his genuine interest in others, his engaging personality, and his advanced listening skills. Kyle Zimmer, an Ashoka board member, said that to be around Drayton is tremendously empowering. His demeanor always makes you feel as if your ideas are heard and will be considered.

Both these examples embody the words of lawyer and media commentator Gerry Spence: "Any really great leader listens" (Adrian, 2001).

Communicating with Actions and Attitude

As should be clear by now, providing leadership requires significantly more communication than simply sending e-mail and memos. The leader's attitude and actions must also be regarded as extremely powerful methods of communication. *Attitude* refers to manners of acting, feeling, or thinking that show one's disposition, opinion, mood, or mental set.

England's Queen Elizabeth I communicated with attitude when she rode into the camp where her army was staging to meet the forces coming their way with the Spanish Armada in 1588. She entered mounted on a magnificent horse, gowned in white, and sporting a silver breastplate. This demonstration of warlike boldness by the "virgin queen" dramatically raised English spirits at a critical historical moment.

Presence, visibility, and availability can have a very strong impact. It communicates that the leader cares about those being led and what they are doing, has an interest in the organization, and has a desire to know what is going on. Being present, visible, and available is also an effective way to get to know your people as human beings and not simply employees.

We all know about the concept of "managing by walking around" (MBWA). I am suggesting the leader try *LBWA:* "leading by wandering around." This means shedding any trace of the detached VIP's arrogant style and taking the time to talk to cadre and other employees. It means both asking and answering questions, and sharing pertinent information.

Few leadership techniques are more communicative than asking open-ended questions—questions whose answer must be more than a simple yes or no. In the course of asking open-ended questions, the leader can not only gather information but also gauge the knowledge, morale, competence, and communication skills of the other person. Are leaders ever oblivious to what the pulse and state of their organization or business unit is? Consider the example of King Louis XVI, the eighteenth-century "absolute monarch" of France. On July 14, 1789, when Parisians stormed the fortress prison known as the Bastille, outside the city he wrote a single word in his daily journal: "*Rien*," meaning "Nothing worth mentioning happened today."

The Positive Influence of Communication

From the foregoing, it should already be obvious that the attribute of effective interpersonal communication multiplies a leader's influence. It is the primary means by which humans relate to one another—leaders to followers and followers to leaders. The more effective the communication, the greater the strength of the bond. Without communication, there is no leadership at all.

In addition, a leader's effective communication validates the cadre of leaders and others who are being led. It transmits a message that the leader cares. Normal human beings will virtually always respond to any form of validation, because it meets their social (highest) need.

The leader's communication casts vision. In doing this it establishes direction, shapes goals and objectives, reinforces key values, and clarifies tasks. It creates a focus and concentration that drives the efforts of everyone on the team, business unit, or within the organization.

Communication also reveals and provides welcome insights about the leader. It can disclose the leader's authenticity, sincerity, genuineness, and virtually every other aspect of a leader's character.

Communication makes the emotional connection that is so critical in effective leadership.

Connecting Attributes

Courage, caring, optimism, self-control, and communication: strong connections run among these five. A synergy forms when a leader develops all of them together.

Hannibal, the Carthaginian general and archenemy of Rome, is one of many historical figures whose power as a leader stemmed from a synergistic combination of attributes. He was personally committed to leading resistance to the Roman empire, and when his generals told him the thirty-two elephants he brought to Europe for the invasion of Rome could not be taken across the Alps in winter, Hannibal used his communicative powers to rally courage and optimism. His line comes down through history: "Find a way or make a way!"

In more recent times as well, leaders' courage will be reflected in both their communication and their optimism. Consider the great classically trained American singer Marian Anderson. Despite racism and rejection, through focus, self-control, and courageous perseverance, she became one of the most popular and critically successful performers in America and overseas. With a repertoire of more than three hundred songs in nine languages, she communicated a message of hope to millions.

A similar synergy is reflected in the life of Margaret Chase Smith, who reached adulthood with only a high school education. When her husband, a Maine representative in the U.S. Congress, died unexpectedly, Smith recalled his advice to put one's whole heart into everything one does, never doing anything halfway. Courageously and with complete optimism, Smith ran for his seat in the U.S. House of Representatives in 1940, won, and served four consecutive terms. Having served as the first woman elected to the House, in 1948 she ran for the Senate and became the first U.S. woman senator as well.

In her first speech in the Senate she courageously spoke directly against Joe McCarthy, Wisconsin's senior senator, and the fear, hate, and suspicion he was promoting. She said the Republican Party should not support that agenda. This 1950 speech communicated the first public denunciation of McCarthy and showed extraordinary courage. It ultimately resulted in the Senate's censure of McCarthy in 1954.

There are more examples, but the principle is clear. If you continuously develop the behaviors related to all five leadership attributes, your behaviors will complement each other and multiply your influence.

In the next chapter, I begin to survey the Five E's: example, experience, education, environment, and evaluation. Each represents a mode or organizational context in which your best attributes and those of your cadre can be developed and sustained.

Building Leadership Character: The Five Attributes

1. In your own experience, what character attributes are most important for leaders? Consider the five in this chapter and any others that you believe a character development process should address.

2. How pertinent are the five leadership attributes to your own leadership style? Do you feel stronger in some than in others?

3. How relevant do these attributes seem to effective leadership in your organization? Are some more present than others?

4. How might the five leadership attributes be applied more effectively to your own leadership behaviors and also more broadly in your work environment?

Chapter Three

Example

Of the Five E's, personal example is probably the most influential and effective tool for developing leadership character in others. Humanitarian Albert Schweitzer went so far as to say, "Example is not the main thing in influencing others. It is the only thing" (E. Anderson, 1981).

Leading by example means having a positive influence on others through your own behavior (actions and attitudes). But your example not only leads, it also develops the leadership capacity of others who study and imitate you.

The Human Urge to Imitate

Simply setting a good example as leader is powerful because the habit of imitating others' behaviors is so ingrained in human nature. This tendency is with us from infancy, and for good reason. Children are impressionable because that is how they learn from parents and from older peers. As a panel from the Guilford Educational Alliance has noted, the best behavioral model for nonadult students is an adult who also exhibits good character (Fernandez, 2005). Leadership development by example begins (or doesn't) early and at home. But the process does not end there, or with leadership character training programs like the Scouts or sports in schools. Throughout life, people tend to imitate four types of behaviors:

- Behaviors of those in authority or positions of power, or those who are popular

- Behaviors they see as desirable, successful, or attractive
- Behaviors they respect, esteem, and value
- Behaviors that allow them to go along with the crowd, conform, and avoid looking different

By and large, often unknowingly, people tend to seek out, appreciate, and emulate what they regard as the positive examples around them, among their leaders in politics or the community or in the news. But note that Schweitzer's view does not say much about the actual content of the behaviors that people tend to imitate. Rather, it speaks in terms of who the model is or how certain behaviors are perceived. Based on your own worldview, value system, and personal vision, you might consider a certain leadership behavior as positive and good. Another person with a different point of view might see that same behavior in a completely opposite way. One leader inspires imitation from one group of people by speaking out against abortion while a different group, advocating the woman's choice, emulates another. Thus an element of choice is always present, both for the person who sets an example and the person who follows it. Leaders must wisely choose how they will behave and then accept the consequences of that behavior, keeping in mind they will never be able to please everyone.

Outstanding Leaders and Their Role Models

Many outstanding and successful leaders have attributed their success to having followed the example of a role model, mentor, parent, or other person they truly respected. They acknowledge being influenced by and consciously emulating the behaviors of that model.

For example, General George S. Patton Jr. served under General of the Armies John J. Pershing both in the 1916–17 punitive campaign against Mexican revolutionary Pancho Villa and again in World War I. He copied Pershing's immaculate style of dress, penchant for details, no-nonsense discipline, and overall professional commitment to the concept of duty. Before Patton deployed for the

EXAMPLE 51

invasion of North Africa in World War II, he went to Walter Reed hospital and knelt to receive a blessing from eighty-three-year-old Pershing. Later, senior officers of the German Army described General Patton as the Allies' most outstanding combat commander. His effectiveness as a combat leader can be attributed in large part to his having followed the example Pershing set as role model and personal hero.

In turn, Patton became my primary icon during my twenty-five years in the army. From him I learned the power of reading to enhance professional competence, the positive influence of an immaculate appearance, the value of direct and honest communication, and the value of appearing confident even when one wasn't. I even went so far as to wear a pinky ring like the general. There were, of course, some very negative sides to General Patton's behaviors, and I made a point to avoid those in my own personal behavior. The lesson is that regardless of whose example we choose to follow, we have to decide which behaviors to emulate and which to avoid.

Rick Warren, author of the spiritual guidance best seller *The Purpose Driven Life* (2002), provides another good example. He is also pastor of the Saddleback Church in Orange County, California, where more than twenty thousand people worship each weekend. He says he was influenced by three men: his father, who was a Baptist pastor; Peter Drucker, whose management techniques Warren has implemented; and Billy Graham, whom Warren views as a perfect example of integrity. Warren also is a voracious reader and has picked up leadership techniques from examples as varied as General Patton and Mohandas Gandhi.

Leading journalist Thomas Friedman—mentioned in Chapter Two and author of the widely acclaimed *The World Is Flat*—has won two Pulitzer Prizes and the 1989 National Book Award for nonfiction. He, too, took advantage of role models. One was Walter Lippman, whom Friedman described as "a reporter and a thinker"; others were William Safire and David Halberstam. He deeply appreciated and modeled their depth of insight, worldview, and communication style. Another major example for Friedman was the former *New York Times* columnist Tom Wicker. The best advice Friedman says he ever got was from Wicker, who told him, "Don't be afraid to be wrong; otherwise you'll never be right" (Brophy, 2005).

Bill Drayton, mentioned earlier as the founder and CEO of Ashoka, says his three heroes are Thomas Jefferson, Jean Monnet (a scholar and political operator, also the architect of Europe's common currency), and Mohandas Gandhi, whom Drayton admires in part for his mania for organization and detail (Hayden, 2005a).

Then there is Juliette Gordon Low, an American advocate of women's suffrage, who was inspired by the example of Sir Robert Baden-Powell, founder of the Boy Scouts. Based on his model and vision, she first organized girl scouts in Britain, then returned to Savannah, Georgia, where she organized what later evolved into the American Girl Scouts organization (Joicey, 2002).

Good Examples Versus Bad

Implicit in developing character through the example of the leader is that, above all, the leader displays and behaves in a way that has a positive and good influence on others. Leaders should exemplify all the traits and qualities that they want their cadre of leadership to have. Essentially, the leader is a role model whom leaders below may choose to follow. Naturally, the cadre will observe the consequences of the leader's behavior, and this will influence their choices.

Unfortunately, many leaders have learned their leadership behavior from an exemplar who was authoritarian, heavy-handed, or relationally challenged. Infamously, for example, Saddam Hussein modeled himself upon the Russian dictator Joseph Stalin. He copied Stalin's terror tactics, Stalin's violence as a leadership strategy, and Stalin's state control mechanisms. Similarly, Juan Perón, the dictator of Argentina (1946 to 1955), was Argentina's military attaché in Italy from 1938 to 1941. In that context, Perón learned much of his fascist behavior from Benito Mussolini. He copied Il Duce's gaudy uniforms, love of parades, and bombastic speaking style.

EXAMPLE   53

Authoritarian behaviors may have application in a crisis, but almost always they have a negative impact during routine operations. Overbearing behaviors generally run counter to achieving commitment and high productivity from employees. Because the authoritarian style is very natural, leaders need to work on and be taught more effective styles. Fortunately, authoritarian behaviors can be overcome by training, practice, and a desire to change. Since these are behaviors that we have a tendency to fall back on when we are frustrated, tired, not feeling well, in a time crunch, or under extreme pressure, we need to constantly assess ourselves to make sure that these types of behavior have not become our normal mode of influence.

This is not to say that a developing leader can't learn from counterexamples. U.S. Army General H. Norman Schwarzkopf said that he learned more from the behaviors of bad leaders than he did from the behaviors of good ones. He learned how not to do some things because he saw the negative reactions, responses, and consequences resulting from certain words and conduct. He avoided the example of the negative leadership he experienced firsthand in the Vietnam War. His opposite behaviors resulted in his extremely successful, victorious leadership in the first Gulf War. But not every junior leader is capable of such discrimination; many will tend to imitate bad senior leaders simply because, as Schweitzer has noted, the senior occupies a position of higher authority.

Developing Character by Your Own Behavioral Example

As this chapter is suggesting, your example helps to develop the leadership potential of those below you. From your patterns of action, your leadership cadre can see for themselves how important consistent behavior is, what behaviors are good and have a positive influence, and what behaviors are bad and do not. In this respect, setting a positive leadership example is really "the highest form of leadership" because of its multiplying effect on other leaders.

The Power of Your Example

Certainly your example carries ten times more power and authority than any book, lecture, or talk with a colleague. Your leadership cadre takes your behaviors as the acceptable standard of conduct.

Your cadre of leaders will actually pick up and imitate your personality traits, mannerisms, and habits—good or bad—based on a number of things. First is the strength of your personality. If you have a personality that "sucks the air out of the room" when you walk in, the probability that your behaviors will have a significant impact is high. Your behavioral example will also have a huge influence on those who have a similar value system, set of professional goals and objectives, and comparable personality type, whether introvert or extravert. Some people have a strong behavioral need to be loyal, supportive, and cooperative to others. This is the high "Wanted Control" interpersonal need on Will Schutz's FIRO-B personality assessment, which was discussed in Chapter One. This need can cause them to follow the behavioral example of the leader. Finally, some members of your leadership cadre will emulate your behaviors simply because you are the boss and they want to stay on your good side and think they may gain some advantage by copying you. Of course, the more consistent, productive, and positive your behaviors are when leading, the higher the probability that they will be copied.

In the course of imitating you, subordinate leaders will tend to use your words, phrases, questions, jokes, favorite sayings, stories, illustrations, and nonverbal gestures. Your energy, enthusiasm, passion, attitudes, flexibility, focus, and priorities will also be emulated. The net result is a need for you to be constantly aware of the extraordinary influence of your behaviors. Other behaviors that will generally be copied are when you come to and leave work, how you handle time, how you treat people, and even how you dress. People will quote you in discussions, explain why something can or can't be done because of how you would react, know what will really

Example   55

please or upset you, and say things like, "Bob will be in real trouble when the boss [meaning you, the leader] finds out what he did!"

The same factors that will cause your cadre of leaders to model your behaviors will come into play between them and their direct reports. Foremost, however, remains strength of personality. This is a combination of natural disposition, experience, and training. Young and inexperienced leaders are by nature tentative and unsure of themselves. Over time, the force of their personality will generally increase as they mature and gain more confidence and experience as a leader. You, as the leader responsible for the development of your cadre's leadership behaviors, must act wisely in how you influence this developmental process. Optimally, you want them to develop their own distinctive personality, leadership style, and behavioral strengths and not just become your clone. On your part, this requires constant observation and assessment of their behaviors and how their leadership attributes are developing.

Handling Your Role as an Example

It's natural for members of your leadership cadre to follow your example. Simply focus on behaving in a constructive, positive, and helpful manner. Don't force others to imitate your behavior or be concerned that they will somehow lose their personality or compromise their own style by mimicking you. Most of your cadre members will pick up on and copy behaviors that they are comfortable with and admire. Only someone who is emotionally unhealthy, or who is trying too hard to be ingratiating, will become your "mini-me." If that occurs, hold a counseling session to get that person refocused.

A good problem to have—but still a challenge, though one that most leaders never have to face—may arise when your behavioral example perfectly fits the personality and temperament of one of your leadership cadre. That leader becomes your greatest disciple, writes down your every word, and wants to please you, working hard at never letting you down. The challenge is to avoid the perception of playing favorites when you respond to this junior leader. It may not be totally possible to avoid this perception, which is actually fine to some degree if the devotee is also a top performer, since all leaders tend to favor their best performers. But be conscious of the perception and avoid overt behaviors that reinforce it.

Suppose you're not one of those naturally highly conspicuous leaders? Should you try to compensate by calling attention to yourself, so that people will notice your exemplary patterns of behavior? My experience is that this is not necessary. If your leadership behaviors are positive, constructive, and beneficial, then not only the members of your leadership cadre but also many others within the organization will notice them. Over time, you—like every other leader—inevitably establish a reputation in your organization. If your behaviors are productive and people-friendly, that will be noted. Along with the quality of your work and the results you achieve, such behaviors speak for themselves. By themselves they will promote you. Let them do it. Deliberate self-promotion can actually have an opposite effect if done poorly, noticeably, or without credible results or behaviors to back it up.

A key element of a truly influential example is believing in or standing for something bigger than yourself. Many people float with the current trends or poll numbers, but as a leader you should evince values that clearly go beyond your personal success and welfare.

Carlos M. Gutierrez, U.S. Secretary of Commerce and former chairman and CEO of Kellogg, supports this notion (Gutierrez, 2005). His experience indicates that if people see a leader looking out only for personal interests, they won't follow the leader. Leaders whose example will be followed are those who believe in doing good for those they serve. This kind of behavior helps subordinates reach their potential, promise, and professional capacity. It allows them to do extraordinary things.

There are effective and ineffective ways to select and promote a value or cause that is greater than yourself. Optimally, as Carlos

EXAMPLE   57

Gutierrez suggests, it should focus on other people. Focusing on the welfare of others is an authentic and workable strategy of leadership. You can select other values beyond yourself, such as promoting the organization or a cause outside the organization, but there are disadvantages to both. Promoting the organization can give you a reputation as a "company man" who has "drunk the Kool Aid" or is simply trying too hard. Taking on a cause that has nothing to do with the organization's mission can earn you the reputation of not having enough to do, being insufficiently committed to the organization, or holding confused priorities. In any event, keep in mind why (in part at least) you are connecting yourself to a greater cause: to model and promote a positive and constructive leadership example that you want others to emulate.

Another challenge in exemplifying good leadership behaviors arises when you make a doozy of a mistake—as most or all of us inevitably do at some point. How does that affect you as an example? I don't mean mistakes like misappropriation of funds, sexual harassment, racial discrimination, threats of violence, and so on that will most likely end your connection to the organization. I mean mistakes of a less odious nature, like bad decisions, mistakes in judgment, poor results on a project, and the like—which are serious enough. The best behavioral example you as the leader can display in these situations is to admit what happened, accept responsibility, share the lessons learned, and continue on. The worst kind of behavior is to shift blame, go into denial, whine or complain, or begin your own personal "pity party." Being resilient means getting up off the ground, shaking yourself off, and moving on. This type of response can *enhance* your image and your personal capital in the company.

Here is one example of how *not* to handle mistakes, from the 2005 season's National Football League playoffs. After his team's 21–18 defeat by the Pittsburgh Steelers, all-pro football quarterback Peyton Manning criticized his offensive line, saying, "I'm trying to be a good teammate here, but let's just say we had some problems in protection. I'll give Pittsburgh credit for their blitzes and their rush, but we did have some problems." According to Scott Soshnick, a Bloomberg news columnist, Manning's comments could be translated as, "I couldn't do my job because the offensive linemen didn't do theirs." Soshnick went on to say that this was "committing one of the ultimate team-sport sins: He assigned blame to someone other than himself. If athletic no-no's were inscribed on stone tablets, 'Thou Shalt Not Blast Your Teammates Publicly' would be high on the list of commandments" (Soshnick, 2006).

At all costs, avoid having a member of your cadre copying one or more of your less-than-positive behaviors. We are all flawed; we all show superficial and potentially negative behaviors. We also display behaviors that may not suit the personality or style of all our cadre members. When a cadre member copies inappropriately, the senior leader needs to have a discussion with that person and explain the concerns the behavior causes. Such open communication is generally very effective in resolving this type of problem. It may also help the senior leader recognize and reshape the personal behavior pattern that inspired the inappropriate emulation, in cases where the behavior was regrettable and not just out of place in the one who copied it.

As a leader, periodically assess and evaluate the example you are setting with your leadership behaviors. The next section assists you in this process. Your answers can lead you to steps to cultivate and sharpen a leadership image that is more influential and has a higher impact.

Assess Yourself as an Example

Take some time to review your own behavior patterns and to take stock of the kind of example you are setting as a leader. Start with the framework of five attributes described in Chapter Two. Then consider any other attributes that seem relevant to your own organization and your own leadership style. Look at both your positive and negative sides of each.

EXAMPLE   59

Also spend some time evaluating what effect your example seems to be having on those around you. It's difficult for all of us, but be as objective and honest with yourself as you can. Begin by asking what have been the *consequences* of your current leadership behaviors—what results have been achieved with them. Examine any feedback you have received about those behaviors. Don't stop with verbal feedback; think also about team members who have left the team, productivity and quality of work, and morale indicators such as excessive complaints, sick leave, or absenteeism. From that assessment you can then make a choice whether you need to adjust or manage your behaviors to be more effective. It may also be helpful to ask yourself the following general questions:

- What image am I projecting with my behavior? Is it the one I want to project?
- Are there other behaviors that I should be emphasizing as a leader? Am I balanced in my behaviors?
- Are my successes making me behave with excessive arrogance, conceit, vanity, or pride? Do I need to be getting more behavioral feedback to ensure they are not?
- Which of my actions set a good example and which set a bad one? How?
- Which of my nonverbal signals, that is, my body language, set a good example and which set a bad one? How?
- Which of my personal mannerisms set a good example and which set a bad one? How?

Performing this type of self-assessment first on yourself should enable you to pass on useful self-assessment advice to more junior leaders in your organization.

Following are some questions you might find useful in assessing yourself as an example with regard to the five basic leadership attributes. Read each one and write down your answers. Try to recall specific instances when your behavior reflected leadership strength, or when you or others were disappointed in how you behaved. Then make a list of your strengths and weaknesses regarding each attribute.

As a concluding activity, as objectively as possible, ask yourself if your behavior in relation to each attribute will enhance your professional career or potentially undermine it. This process is an excellent start for building on your behavioral strengths and improving areas of weakness.

Courage

- How aggressively do you tackle controversial or politically charged issues?
- What causes you to hesitate when you know you should take action?
- Do you consider yourself decisive? Why or why not?
- Do you continually ask for more information in order to make a decision? At what point do you feel you have enough information?
- What comfort level do you have in standing up for your values and beliefs even when they conflict with those of your boss, your boss's boss, or the organization? How prone are you to take risks? Have you ever been courageous to a fault and, like Colonel Custer at the Little Big Horn, made what could be considered a rash decision?
- How would the various members of your cadre of leaders answer these questions about you? Why?
- In the area of courage, does their behavior model yours?

Caring

- Do your actions and attitudes consistently indicate that people are important?
- Do you model sincere interest and genuine concern in the values, interests, and hobbies of your cadre members?

EXAMPLE **61**

- From your behaviors are you considered an employee-friendly leader?
- Do you make a priority of treating people with respect and dignity?
- Are your behaviors toward others considered genuine and authentic or manipulative and self-serving?
- Do you at times do something positive for one person that is actually at the expense of someone else?
- Do you balance achieving the desired results with the impact the effort will have on your leadership cadre?
- What about your model of handling people issues is worthy of emulation by your cadre members?

Optimism

- Are you generally viewed as being positive, upbeat, and having a can-do attitude? Do you operate under the philosophy that the glass is half full or half empty?
- Do you see opportunities and silver linings in the problems and difficulties that arise?
- Do you put the best construction on everything? Do people like to be around you because your behavior is constructive, helpful, supportive, and accommodating?
- Have you ever been optimistic to the point that you were accused of not being in touch with reality or knowing what was really going on?
- Has the political nature of any of your jobs ever required you be optimistic even though the facts and indicators did not support such optimism?
- Do you ever tend to behave in a negative, pessimistic, downbeat, skeptical, and cynical manner? Do certain persons or events trigger such behavior in you?
- Like the news media, do you use provocative behavior as a managerial technique?

Self-Control

- Is your behavior highly self-disciplined?
- Are your personal habits worthy of emulation by your leadership cadre in the areas of eating, drinking, physical exercise, and stress management?
- Do your work ethic and work habits provide a positive model for your leadership cadre?
- Are there certain people or situations at work that upset you and perhaps even have caused you to temporarily lose control of your temper? If so, what does that look like and what do you do to regain your balance?
- Have your behaviors earned you the reputation of being consistent whether things are going well or not? Are you a pillar of strength and stability when everyone else around you is losing it?
- Is there even the slightest hint of impropriety in your conduct in the areas of sex, drugs, gambling, or the management of organizational funds?
- Will the lack of self-control displayed in your personal lifestyle cause you to lose promotion or other professional opportunities, as baseball legend Babe Ruth's excesses did?

Communication

- Would those who work with and for you describe your listening skills as effective and well above average?
- What signals and messages do your nonverbal behaviors communicate? How do you know? Do people see what you are thinking even when you are not saying anything?
- Do you make a conscious effort to keep your leadership cadre well informed? What do you not communicate that you should? In what situations have you overcommunicated?

EXAMPLE 63

- Are you considered an effective facilitator of meetings or small groups?
- How effective are you when speaking to several hundred people or as the master of ceremonies of the annual company awards banquet?
- Is your ability to communicate in writing well developed? Is your writing style clear, succinct, and to the point? Have you ever published a professional article?
- Are you known as an effective leader because of your ability to communicate?
- Do you ever use inappropriate, coarse, or vulgar language?
- Have you ever received any feedback on whether or not your verbal communication indicated you have a high or low emotional intelligence?

As I discuss in more detail in Chapter Seven, feedback is the best means to understand the impact, influence, and effectiveness of your leadership behaviors. If you are truly interested in understanding the behavioral example you are setting, share these questions with your boss, a peer, and various members of your leadership cadre to find out how they see you. Candid verbal feedback and honest behavioral feedback from 360-degree assessments can be the best foundation for any development process for leadership character.

Of the Five E's, example comes first because it is the most powerful and has the highest potential for impact. In the next chapter I turn to experience, generally the second most effective for developing leadership character. As with example, experience will be discussed in the context of the five leadership attributes that are crucial to effective leadership: courage, caring, optimism, self-control, and communication.

Building Leadership Character: Example

1. Why do people generally follow the example of others? Do you see these forces at work in your organization? Write down some examples.

2. What leaders or role models do you strive to emulate or live up to? How?

3. How pertinent does leadership development by example seem to your own leadership style and to the organizational culture where you work?

4. Do examples of good leadership strongly outweigh mediocre or bad examples in your organization? If not, what seems to be the problem?

5. Are there ways that good examples of leadership could be made more conspicuous or more prestigious in your organization—and therefore more likely to be copied?

6. What work could you be doing to set a better example as a leader?

Chapter Four

Experience

After example, experience is the next best avenue for the character development of leaders. In this context, experience refers to learning from life circumstances, events, and relationships. It is the sum total of all that has happened in the leader's life to date; it is the resulting impact of everything the leader has done or undergone.

Courage, caring, optimism, self-control, and communication can all develop through experience. For example, I was a battalion commander of six hundred paratroopers for two years, including deployment to Desert Shield and Desert Storm. I learned many things from this leadership experience, but foremost was the priceless value of effective communication. The experience validated and reinforced many of the leadership behaviors that I had already been practicing, and it taught me some new ones as well.

Casey Stengel, whose New York Yankees baseball teams won seven World Series, understood the value of experience. As a matter of routine, he sought out older, more experienced players and added them to the Yankees roster. Other teams had generally given up on these players because of their age. Stengel, however, recognized that with age came a vast amount of experience that he could use to advantage. In another type of entertainment, the producers of the hit TV sitcom *The Love Boat* routinely had older, semiretired actors and actresses on the series. The experience these professionals brought was one of the things that made the series such a huge success.

What makes experience essential to leadership character development, and how can you ensure that your junior leaders benefit from experience? Let's begin by saying more about the basic useful-ness of experience.

The Basic Value of Experience

William James, who is regarded as America's first psychologist, was the leading exponent of American pragmatism. A basic idea behind this school of thought was that truth could be derived only from ex-perience (Joicey, 2002).

Reading or being told of others' experiences does have value, but nothing compares with undergoing something personally. As the saying goes, nothing is real to you unless you experience it; oth-erwise it is just hearsay.

My work as an executive education trainer confirms this. I can share the most profound and well-researched leadership information with my class, and the information makes no impact on some partic-ipants who have not experienced it firsthand. This happens particu-larly when we discuss the value of treating employees with respect, trust, dignity, affirmation, validation, acceptance, and care. Many executives have a "results first" mentality; to them, people are noth-ing but another resource from which to get results. Without experi-encing it directly, they simply reject strong evidence that respectful treatment is likely to get better results.

A second major value of experience is that it expands a leader's knowledge base, expertise, proficiency, and skill levels. It increases wisdom, understanding, maturity, resilience, credibility, and confi-dence. Experience is also valuable because it improves efficiency, re-duces the time to accomplish a task, enhances self-esteem, and shows the value of having and communicating a vision and of goal setting. In addition, experience provides new perspectives on val-ues, priorities, relationships, and success. It is through experiences, both personal and professional, that we clarify and validate our val-ues. Experience can also provide the hopeful teaching that it may never be too late to become what we want to be.

Through expanded experience specifically in leading, you and your cadre can personally determine good leadership behaviors that actually work, fit your individual style, and are appropriate to specific situations. You learn what leadership behaviors are good or bad, and the consequences of each. You learn which behaviors to repeat in the future and which ones to avoid. Over time, repeating positive leadership behaviors also increases your proficiency at using them.

Experience can also confront you with incipient behaviors that have the potential to derail your career. Through experience, you can adjust your behavior to achieve a higher impact overall. This is really the ultimate purpose of understanding the impact of leadership behaviors.

However, implied in all this is that the leader actually learns from circumstances, events, and relationships. This requires reflecting on what happened, its impact, and what can be learned. It requires introspection about individual impressions, reactions, thoughts, and feelings, and becoming more self-aware of why we react to things as we do. It is not unusual for a person to undergo an experience but miss learning from it. An unaware leader can have twenty years of experience that amount to repeating the same experiences twenty times. As the German king Frederick the Great said, a donkey may have participated in ten military campaigns but when all is said and done, it is still a donkey.

Beyond awareness of what has happened, learning from experience entails applying new learning to future situations and relationships. It means putting information into practice. Without application, there really is no learning. Head-only knowledge—even from experience—is pedantry and sophistry rather than learning in the truest sense.

The rest of this chapter deals with four topics. First, it tells how you and your cadre can develop good leadership behaviors in the course of challenging job assignments, participation in task forces, special projects, committees, multifunctional teams, and so on. Then it describes three key areas of learning in which challenging experiences are especially instructive. Third, the chapter discusses how a leader can learn from *other* leaders' experience. Finally, it explores how leaders can develop positive leadership behaviors through adversity and hardships such as business mistakes, career setbacks, and other personal traumas.

Developing Good Leadership Behaviors with Challenging Job Assignments

Since leaders spend less than 1 percent of their time in the classroom, learning (especially of leadership behaviors) takes place primarily at the workplace and from job assignments (McCall, Lombardo, & Morrison, 1988). In the business world, some jobs and assignments are extremely challenging and carry great responsibility, whereas others are more likely to be routine. By placing junior leaders in challenging positions, you can stimulate their development of behaviors that are positive and influential. As you may be aware, some corporations already make extensive use of this technique.

Good Developmental Assignments

All jobs can have a developmental component, but stretch assignments are the most valuable as developers of leadership behaviors and character. The U.S. Army recognizes this in its experiential model of leadership development. It gives officers a variety of challenging assignments because the responsibilities and risks associated with them and their positive behavioral requirements are highly developmental. Unless already serving in an upper-level staff position, during peacetime an officer does not stay in one position for more than two years, and the time is often less. Since every transfer entails a learning curve, this movement of officer personnel lessens immediate organizational efficiency, but the army consciously accepts this as a price of leadership development.

Research from the Center for Creative Leadership indicates that difficult assignments are excellent teachers for high-potential developing leaders. Senior leaders invariably say they learned the most in assignments where the stakes were highest. To be completely accurate, it is not the assignment that develops character but what the assignment requires the leader to do (McCall, Lombardo, & Morrison, 1988). An assignment that requires integrating numerous skills and behaviors is likely to be the best one for developing consistent and influential leadership behavior.

New experience teaches. When you place developing leaders in new and unfamiliar job circumstances, learning automatically takes place. People quickly recognize that they have no choice but to deal with the problems at hand, even if it is not really clear how. Leaders in these situations develop because they must and not necessarily because they want to. They are forced to learn because the challenge is for real and everyone else is playing for keeps. They readily see the necessity and benefits of taking the initiative. In these circumstances, they seek out information and details about the problems they face; they act and make needed adjustments to achieve desired results; they learn what they can, when they can, and from whatever sources they have. Doing so is clearly in their best interests, as a practical matter of survival. For many leaders this process and the behaviors involved are exhilarating and exciting, almost like a form of corporate combat.

Individuals with the highest leadership potential take responsibility for their own learning and behaviors because their success and future opportunities require it. Stretch job assignments are powerful teachers because they confirm success by rewarding success. Challenging jobs are also beneficial because, as leaders increase in competence, their confidence in themselves and their abilities grows; they become tougher and more independent, which subsequently encourages and motivates them to take on even more difficult problems (McCall, Lombardo, & Morrison, 1988). Most important, they learn which of their leadership behaviors are positive and effective and which are not.

Encouraging Leaders Through Stretch Assignments

Learning from a stretch assignment is a process with which you as senior leader can significantly assist.

For example, virtually all stretch assignments require some additional or new technical knowledge. Peter Drucker, the father of modern management, always advised managers to focus on one task or requirement at a time (Drucker, 1967). This is excellent and proven advice for leaders as well, but unfortunately, developing leaders seldom follow it when they are left to their own devices. Your guidance can be crucial here. If a new job exposes gaps in skills or knowledge, you can encourage the developing leader to concentrate on learning one technical area at a time. The sequence of learning depends on the job, but to simultaneously study market research, financial planning and analysis, the detail of product development and its associated research, and also the current strategic plans is setting oneself up for failure.

Another way to assist junior leaders is to steer them away from attempting to make a large immediate impact. Developing leaders may make dramatic operational changes even though the division of which they are now in charge is doing well. Such changes are usually poorly received, as the leader painfully learns. There are usually sound reasons why things are being done as they are. New leaders need to consider those reasons even when they see what appears to be a new and better way.

For this reason, a senior leader should encourage those in stretch assignments to get input from the workforce that will be affected by the change and to be aware of people's level of commitment. If commitment is low, the change is unlikely to work, and new leaders are likely to be seen as loose cannons who think they know it all and do not listen to others. It takes some leaders months to recover from this type of initial error; some report that they never recovered.

However, even a developing leader who is not sure what to do—and sees no immediate room for large change—should be taught and encouraged to do something. Something positive almost always comes from well-conceived, proactive behavior. Conversely, something negative generally results from passively doing nothing. By their very nature, developmental job assignments involve risk and require action. Taking action also carries risk, but the risk of inaction is generally greater. In the military people say, "Do something even if it is wrong." The principle inherent in this bit of hyperbole is that in most situations the momentum that results from doing something and not just sitting around will remove obstacles, eradicate impasses, and cause positive things to happen.

Leaders in developmental assignments should be encouraged to consistently stay proactive and exercise initiative. Stretch jobs do not allow the leader to sit back and watch and wait. The leader has to get involved. Not to do so is a setup for failure.

Proactive behavior means anticipating what could go wrong and then acting accordingly. Thinking preventively can help the developing leader to avoid significant mistakes, embarrassment, and derailment.

The Social Learning of Stretch Assignments

Probably the biggest revelations for leaders in developmental assignments have to do with other people. Although developing strong interpersonal leadership skills is not usually a priority for pure managers, administrators, or bureaucrats, it is essential for leaders. It is sometimes easy to forget the importance of interpersonal relationships at work, but relationships are the glue of organizations. In stretch assignments, members of your leadership cadre should be strongly encouraged to focus on interpersonal relationship skills. This is also a good area for coaching on your part.

Developmental assignments invariably demand the ability to understand people and develop strong relationships. Other people always need to be taken into account. The key attribute here is often caring. Caring is never a waste of time. Huge and very costly lessons may come from ignoring, marginalizing, or mistreating others.

In your role as senior leader, ensure that your developing leaders understand the importance of motivating and relying on others rather than doing the job themselves. Encourage and assist them in developing their powers of persuasion and influence. They may need to learn new processes for selecting, placing, replacing, hiring, and terminating employees. Inevitably, employee performance and conduct problems need to be confronted. Tolerating ineffective subordinates whose performance is mediocre or conduct objectionable always causes a great loss of influence for leaders, and especially for developing leaders. These types of challenges can be among the most difficult for a new leader to handle, but others will be watching closely how and how well the leader performs. Your leaders may also need to work on skills related to coaching, networking, mentoring, dealing with people over whom they have no formal authority, and understanding diverse points of view. You, their leader, have a major responsibility to ensure that each of your cadre of leaders receives the needed leadership training, coaching, and feedback to do all these things well.

Another area that a senior leader may need to monitor has to do with the fact that developmental assignments often include contract or joint venture negotiations with potential partners, customers, clients, suppliers, and so on. Negotiation with challenging elements such as unions, activists, influence groups, the news media, and even foreign governments may also be part of a leader's new responsibilities. Success with all of these depends heavily on a leader's relational skills and behaviors. A senior leader needs to make sure that the skills are there.

Stretch positions generally also require the developing leader work with and be highly visible to senior management. Junior leaders may need to give presentations on data or topics about which they have only surface knowledge. The senior leader may need to help them develop behaviors that allow them to persuade their seniors, present contrary opinions effectively, and act confidently and credibly, even when they are not very experienced and what they need to say runs counter to corporate traditions or procedures or management's guidance or preference. The developing leader may need to go out on a limb in front of a group that could ask any number of questions that are difficult to answer—and not just senior leaders within the organization, but external parties such as customers, competitors, suppliers, government regulators, Wall Street analysts, or activist groups. Since this is something no one learns effectively in school, you will probably need to guide and train them to behave in these situations with polish and finesse (McCall, Lombardo, & Morrison, 1988).

Young professionals soon realize that their expensive formal education has not taught them everything they need to know for success. Organizations can be an entirely new world regardless of someone's previous experience or where they interned. Knowing the right answer is only 10 percent of the battle; working with people is the other 90 percent (McCall, Lombardo, & Morrison, 1988). And *knowing* the right people is just as important at times as working hard.

The social challenges of stretch assignments also include learning to cope with ambiguity and understanding and fitting in with the organization's vision, strategy, and culture. In these job assignments, developing leaders' personal value system must mesh with the organizational value system. Invariably, new leaders will form new values as some of their preexisting values prove no longer relevant. Most of the time, this is a natural and routine process, but it can become a challenge when major conflict arises between the value systems of a leader and the organization. In such instances, you as senior leader must invest the time to help the developing leader reconcile the two. Inevitably you will have insights to impart about the corporate value system.

Promoting a Habit of Professional Reading

Finally, in connection with a stretch assignment, encourage your leadership cadre to take on a serious program of professional reading.

No matter what the focus of an assignment, published information is available offering useful managerial tips, leadership insights, and technical data. Developing leaders often need to be encouraged to take advantage of it. There are limits to how much a person can experience directly. Vicarious experience through reading helps to fill the gaps.

Types of Stretch Assignments

Various types of professional experiences can help to develop leadership behaviors, such as being in charge of a special project, serving in an interim or lateral position, undergoing cross-training, or joining a task force, work group, committee, or multifunctional team. Assignments or responsibilities can extend beyond the leader's normal job description. Good in this regard are co-leaderships or temporary assistantships with other teams, and lateral moves. Ed Zander, chairman and CEO of Motorola, supports this idea (Zander, 2005). He believes the key to business success is innovation and breaking things up. One way to break things up is to move junior leaders and others around. This changes the company's organizational structure, allows different people to interact and share ideas with one another, and lets new ideas grow and take shape.

In conjunction with human resources and other organizational leaders, leadership cadre members can be exchanged with other business units or put on temporary loan so they can receive additional developmental opportunities. The downside of this is temporarily giving up people and taking the chance that you might be giving them up for good. The upside is that other high-potential leaders will be joining your team.

In this context, highly developmental experiences include moving from line to staff (or from staff to line), positions with increased or largely different scope of responsibilities, expatriate assignments, and taking over a new or troubled project. All of these, by their nature, greatly assist an individual leader to further develop leadership behaviors that have a positive influence on others. While risk is unavoidable, succeeding in these types of jobs reinforces good leadership behaviors and helps eliminate bad ones. It can produce great learning, enhance confidence, and move individuals closer to fulfilling their potential.

Three Areas of Gain from Experiential Learning

Developmental assignments contribute to many areas of learning, but three stand out: dealing with ambiguity and uncertainty, having a strong work ethic, and handling stress. As with everything else that has been mentioned so far in this chapter, it is expected that the leader responsible for the development process has already done the work of personal development in these areas and is continuing that development. This is necessary not just to set a positive example but also to be able to coach and share experiences.

Dealing with Ambiguity and Uncertainty

First, your cadre of leaders must learn to deal with ever-rising levels of ambiguity and uncertainty. At lower-level staff or supervisory positions, the information needed to do a job well is easily available. Developmental and stretch assignments never come with all required information at hand. In positions of increased scope and responsibility, ability to acquire information becomes increasingly important. Many times, inexperienced leaders do not know where to obtain the information they need. For them, learning how to locate and gather information must become a priority. Often, it will be a matter of survival. But escaping the mind-set that more information is always needed is another important step in the move from a lower-level job to a higher-level executive position. Developing leaders need to learn how to focus on gathering the types of information that clarify what is important and separate issues that need available resources from secondary and tertiary issues.

Strong Work Ethic

Be sure to impress your cadre of leaders with the fact that developmental assignments invariably demand a strong work ethic. Ivan Seidenberg, chairman and CEO of Verizon, constantly tells his employees that hard work opens doors (Seidenberg, 2005). His message is to work hard, have high standards, and stick to your values, because somebody's always watching.

Experience shows that leaders who lack a strong work ethic have an exceptionally difficult time with stretch assignments. Stretch jobs demand high effort, high energy, and extended application. Often, the developing leader does not start out with the knowledge and skills required. New, self-taught skills and knowledge must often be acquired virtually overnight (McCall, Lombardo, & Morrison, 1988).

A consistent pattern of working hard can be highly positive and influential. Roger Ailes, chairman and CEO of Fox News Channel, points out the need to provide real value to whomever you are working for (Hayden, 2005b). Most everyone respects hard workers and resents those who are slothful. Hard work creates luck, creates opportunity, develops individual talents, and helps leaders reach their full potential. More than any other one thing, it guarantees vocational effectiveness. Hard work can make up for lack of talent, ability, education, or social background. As a German proverb neatly puts it, "Genius is work"—and the anonymous tipster who said that the secret of success is simply working harder than the other guy was onto something. Fortunately, that is one factor that the developing leader can control. Maybe Lance Armstrong was on to something: anyone may claim to want to succeed, but few are willing to put in the required work, effort, and sacrifice.

Working hard means working smart—not just more hours. This includes using others' expertise, delegating, empowering, hiring employees who can cover weaknesses, managing circumstances over which you have no real control, and deferring situations that can be dealt with in the future if at all.

Working hard also means using time wisely, since time is one of a leader's most valuable resources. Diligence does not mean being a workaholic or spending a hundred hours a week on the job. It means doing what you have to do when you have to do it. Diligence means setting priorities, being able to say no, placing secondary issues in proper perspective, and not losing sight of the vision. It is taking each task and asking oneself, "What is the most important thing to do right now?" When that is determined, a leader can step in and do what needs to be done today, letting tomorrow worry about itself.

Managing Stress

Developmental assignments demand an ability to manage stress and the pressures inherent in results-driven performance. Both the stakes and the risks are invariably high. The leader's decisions may determine the survival of the project, the product, or even the business unit. Stress may also stem from unreasonable deadlines and ultimatums, high financial risks, threats regarding the consequences of failure, a shortage of key resources, and a lack of information.

Stretch jobs customarily call on behaviors reflecting decisiveness, willingness to take risk, guts, and a high sense of responsibility. This constellation of qualities is not at all common. A developing leader's lack of one or more of them can cause significant stress. A further source of stress is the number of factors beyond the control of the developing leader. In lower-level positions leaders typically had a great deal of direct control over what they were doing. By its nature, a developmental assignment means much less control.

A leader's superiors, peers, and direct reports will closely observe the manner in which the developing leader handles stress and pressure. If the leader's pattern of behavior and demeanor reveal an inability to handle stress, that will become apparent to all and will significantly reduce the leader's positive influence and overall promotion potential.

As a senior leader, you can coach your developing leaders on behaviors that would help them handle stress effectively, including helping them identify their sources of stress and creating their own set of stress relievers. Good stress relievers are complete diversions from the work, as well as being activities that do not produce stresses of their own. The idea is to completely remove the pressures and strains produced by work. Activities can include reading, watching movies, fishing, gardening, or a wide variety of similar hobbies. President Franklin D. Roosevelt reduced stress during World War II and the Great Depression by collecting stamps. I can remove myself from all stress by reading a good historical novel or social history. You can also help ensure that your cadre of leaders exercise regularly—jogging, swimming, cycling, lifting weights, or even walking. Exercise is a top stress reliever. Allowing work time in which to exercise can be a huge incentive. Exercising together as a team has also been very effective at SPX Corporation and many other organizations.

Your leadership cadre should also be encouraged to volunteer for projects that help others. This is another proven method to reduce stress. It shifts one's focus from oneself to persons in need. Leaders can be encouraged to become involved in a Habitat for Humanity project, a Big Brother or Big Sister program, a soup kitchen, or the like. Serving others is really a high form of serving oneself. I know from my own experience I always feel better about myself after I perform any kind of good deed for someone else.

Leaders should also ensure their cadre understand how important diet is to stress reduction. A healthy and fiber-rich diet, drinking plenty of fluids and a low to moderate caffeine intake daily, and moderate eating are all effective stress reducers. Getting seven hours of sleep every night can also contribute to stress reduction.

Learning Leadership Behaviors from the Experience of Other Leaders

Your leadership cadre can learn not only from their own experience but also from the experiences of others. By doing this they can avoid many mistakes and some of the difficult teachings of "the school of hard knocks."

Experiencing "the Boss"

As suggested in Chapter Three, your junior leaders will learn a considerable amount from observing or hearing about your behaviors and experience. Research from the Center for Creative Leadership revealed that 20 percent of all key events in the careers of executives featured a boss rather than a job assignment. It was the immediate boss and not the various business situations that was the primary force behind the learning in key events (McCall, Lombardo, & Morrison, 1988). In *The Human Side of Enterprise*, Douglas McGregor ([1960] 2005) suggests that every encounter with a boss reinforces or modifies the attitudes, habits, or expectations of a subordinate. Personal encounters clearly show the developing leader what you, the boss, really stand for.

From you, your cadre of leaders can learn different approaches to a wide variety of situations and circumstances. If alert and observant, they learn from both your strengths and your weaknesses. In this way, you can be a major influence and can teach what cannot be taught by assignments. Lessons learned from a senior leader complement, balance, and support lessons learned from job assignments. One of a leadership cadre's biggest learnings from you, the leader, can be how to behave, operate, and influence so as to get results within the value system of the organization.

Biography as Shared Experience

Another valuable mode of access to the experience of other leaders—especially great ones—is biography and autobiography. From this type of reading, leaders can learn how to avoid many serious mistakes. They can also look for ways to apply the effective, positive behaviors that underpin a great leader's success.

If you are going to read one book of biographical studies, make it Senator John McCain's *Character Is Destiny* (2005). It provides biographical sketches of great leaders who through courage, perseverance, and hard work overcame adversity and had a huge impact on their times and society. Admiral Lord Nelson, Mohandas Gandhi, Viktor Frankl, and Sir Ernest Shackleton are some of the people McCain discusses. If you are interested solely in business leaders, Neil Hamilton's 1999 two-volume *American Business Leaders: From Colonial Times to the Present* is an informative place to start. It includes the biographies of more than four hundred visionary leaders who had a significant impact on American society, including George Westinghouse, the four Warner brothers, Andrew Carnegie, Henry Ford, Calvin Klein, Debbie Fields, Jann Wenner, and Ben Cohen of Ben and Jerry's. These books are a good investment to make on behalf of your leadership cadre.

Biographies and the Five Basic Attributes

It's especially helpful to select biographies of leaders who were strong in terms of the basic attributes: courage, caring, optimism, self-control, and communicational skills. These attributes are universally and cross-culturally relevant, and they are essentially timeless.

The life of Napoleon Bonaparte, French emperor and military leader extraordinaire, offers much food for thought about courage, such as the following incident in which Napoleon was able to translate his own enormous courage into greater courage among his men. During the French Revolution of 1793, the British and Spanish had occupied the French port of Toulon in support of the counterrevolutionary royalist French government. Napoleon, then an unknown artillery captain, was placed in charge of the French revolutionary artillery unit that opposed the occupation. In his reconnaissance, Napoleon noted that a primary site for one of his artillery batteries was a certain hill overlooking the enemy's garrison. However, the hill was within enemy rifle range, so none of Napoleon's artillerymen wanted to man those guns.

With his great sense of psychology, Napoleon placed a sign by the battery that read, "This gun is manned by the bravest of the brave." Then he is reported to have said to his men, "I'm going to create a battery of fearless men. I need men, real men. I insist that they follow me to that position. If you are one of those men, raise your hand" (Weider, n.d.). They all raised their hands, then lifted both arms into the air and shouted, *"Vive Bonaparte."* Thereafter, Napoleon always had enough volunteers to man those guns, and the battery was named "The Men Without Fear." Ultimately, this battery played a key role in the French victory of the Battle of Toulon. The event resulted in a promotion for Napoleon and began his rise to power. (See Chandler, 1973, for an excellent book on Napoleon as leader.)

Biography can also convey the importance of caring in a great leader's career. A high form of caring about others is actually raising them to a higher level of performance. For nine years, Vince Lombardi coached the Green Bay Packers football team (Maraniss, 1999). In 1958, the year prior to Coach Lombardi's arrival, the Packers had a record of one win, ten losses, and a tie. Three years later, in 1961, the Packers won the National Football League championship. Fourteen of the twenty-two starters on the championship team had been on that dismal team of 1958. Lombardi's biography shows how his developmental leadership techniques and behaviors raised their performance to championship level.

Lombardi believed in his players and was convinced that everyone has considerable untapped potential. No matter how awkward and unpolished a player looked from the outside, Lombardi made an effort to see more deeply and envision the player's fullest possibility. He recognized that one of his highest responsibilities was to develop his players' capacities for greatness and help them to "be all they could be."

Lombardi's caring leadership was grounded in the well-understood but seldom emphasized principle that people will respond in proportion to our expectations of them. One result was that the players reciprocated by authenticating Lombardi as *their* leader. Another result was that there are now more players in the Pro Football Hall of Fame from Lombardi's team than from any other team in the history of professional football.

Other effective leaders are also worth reading about for understanding caring leadership as leadership that develops others. One candidate is Steve Jobs, the CEO of Apple, whose encouraging and supportive leadership behaviors have positively transformed the abilities of his cadre.

Biography is also a great way to understand the power of a leader's optimism. In 1914 Sir Ernest Shackleton set off with an expedition to cross the South Polar continent from sea to sea. He did not achieve it, but his optimism and never-say-die attitude left such a legacy that some rate him among the best leaders of all time.

In a first great mishap, his ship, the *Endurance*, was trapped by ice in the Weddell Sea for ten months and was eventually crushed, but Shackleton's optimistic attitude and behaviors kept everyone's hopes alive. According to crewmember Frank Worsley, "Despite this major reverse Sir Ernest showed great leadership in keeping up the morale of the team. One would think he never had a care on his mind and he is the life and soul of half the skylarking and fooling in the ship" (Shackleton, [1926] 1992). Another crewmember, the doctor Alexander Macklin, added that when Shackleton came across you by yourself, he had a nice way of getting into conversation and talking to you in an intimate sort of way.

The crew then lived on an ice floe for almost five months, drifting the entire time around the South Atlantic. Finally, in whaleboats they salvaged from the *Endurance*, they reached deserted Elephant Island. From there, Shackleton and five companions set out in an open boat to seek help at a Norwegian whaling station on South Georgia, another island eight hundred miles away. In an extraordinary feat of navigation they reached the island, only to find out they had landed on the wrong side. Reaching the whaling station meant crossing glaciers several thousand feet high. Again, through Shackleton's optimism, determination, and leadership genius they got there. After four attempts, his twenty-two men left at Elephant Island were also rescued. Through this entire event not one expedition life was lost. Sixty years after the event, the expedition's first officer, Lionel Greenstreet, was asked how they had survived such an adventure. His one-word answer: "Shackleton." Shackleton must have understood all five leadership attributes very well. Such was the result of one leader's optimism, positive nature, can-do attitude, and supportive, encouraging leadership style.

The life of George Washington is an excellent study in self-control. In his early days, Washington was known for a temper that exploded each time he was questioned or criticized. He eventually realized that to meet his goals and the personal vision he held of himself, he would have to increase his self-control. As with everything, he put himself into this with all his strength. Believing correctly that human nature could be continuously improved, he devoted himself to self-improvement. He resolved not to overreact or react badly to criticism. He further determined to become a person of integrity. Through hard work he restrained his behaviors and appetites and became a man of character and a perfect gentleman, able to remain calm and focused in any situation. Even when the war was going poorly and the lack of support from the Continental Congress was frustrating, he was able to remain calm. Through the constant application of self-control he won a great military victory, was the unanimous choice to become the first president, and later received the deserved title of father of his country (McCain, 2005). A reader can learn from Washington's experience not only that controlling one's own behavior is valuable for oneself, but also that good can come to others through that self-control.

With regard to communication, much can be learned from the life of someone like Admiral Lord Horatio Nelson, the greatest British naval commander (White, 2005). Known for "the Nelson touch," he was a master communicator, inspiring and communicating to his men through words and even more through gestures. In all his naval battles he would stand exposed on the quarterdeck as an inspiration to his sailors. In 1794, he lost his right eye. During the Battle of Cape St. Vincent in 1797, a canister of Spanish grapeshot shattered Nelson's right arm. It was amputated without anesthesia and shortly thereafter Nelson was back directing the battle. Obviously a sign of great physical courage, it was also a definite message that he expected his fleet to win.

During the Battle of Copenhagen in 1801, Nelson's commander, Admiral Hyde Parker, signaled him to break off the battle and sail out of gun range. In response, Nelson put his telescope to his blind eye and said that he could not make out his commander's signal. The battle continued and ended in victory for Nelson. But more to the point here, what he communicated by his telescope gesture made him a legend in the British navy. Among other things, Nelson's experience is an important reminder that actions often speak louder than words.

Developing Good Leadership Behaviors from Hardship and Adversity

Research from the Center for Creative Leadership confirms that of all leadership learning from experience, the greatest learning (34 percent) occurs from hardships (Douglas, 2003). Joan Rivers got it right when she said that if we study the lives of great men and women carefully and unemotionally we find that, invariably, greatness was developed, tested, and revealed through the darker periods of their lives (Munier, 2004). (Rivers adds that her comedy routines come out of her own personal unhappiness.)

Professional hardships can arise from many types of experience:

- Major or continuous change
- Being downsized or downsizing others
- Being terminated or terminating others
- Business or project failures
- Financial losses
- Poor subordinate performance, conduct problems, or otherwise difficult employees

- Litigation
- Hostile takeover or being lost in a merger
- Demotions, missed promotions
- Working in a dead-end job or being transferred to an undesirable one
- Failure to take advantage of opportunities
- Business mistakes in which your judgment and decisions resulted in a debacle
- Conflicts that got out of hand

Other common hard experiences are strikes, employee violence, industrial accidents, natural disasters, organizational scandals, personal trauma, and all sorts of career setbacks.

The Benefits of Hardship

Adversity and hardship contribute to character development when they cause personal reflection and introspection about a leader's behaviors and influence. Hardship can cause leaders to look inside themselves, asking questions the answers to which can result in huge learnings and behavioral adjustments. Hardship can reveal a leader's behavioral blind spots, inconsistencies, weaknesses, personal limitations, and ineffective or bad behaviors. Hardship can show a leader how life may be out of balance if too much emphasis has been placed on professional activity and too little on other relationships.

Hardship and adversity can also be cleansing. They can have a refining effect. Through suffering, the dross of one's personality can be removed. It can cause a leader to look at personal behavioral challenges related to anger, impatience, fear, selfishness, and so on. Adversity can also produce a clearer focus and concentration on what is important in life and what is not. After the terrorist attack of 9/11, many of the survivors indicated they now realized how fragile life is and how important relationships are and work is not.

There is also a maturing element to hardship. *Mature* means being seasoned, tested, hardened, weathered, ready, and fully developed.

This maturing effect is often evident in an experience of war. An Australian acquaintance tells the story of a schoolboy friend who served in the Australian army in the anticommunist campaign in Malaysia in the late 1950s. He says that the result of the friend's wartime experience was a complete and positive change of personality. Prior to the war he'd been doing many of the frivolous things young men do. When he returned, he was more mature, focused, and liberated from youthful behaviors. Thus, adversity and hardships can take each of us to a higher level of character development.

A major learning from hardship can be the value of relationships. As with some developmental assignments, many professional hardships result from a failure to deal effectively with other people. Poor personal relationships may not be the cause of many personal hardships, but they have the potential to compound or amplify them.

Dealing with Poor Reactions to Hardship

Of course, some cadre members will not view their professional or personal hardship experience as something positive and replete with opportunities. Instead they become bitter, sour, and angry. How should the senior leader handle this? Are there preventive measures? This is where caring and communication play another key role. Optimally you as leader should communicate words of understanding, support, empathy, and even sympathy. In the case of a personal tragedy like a death or broken relationship it is totally appropriate to ask people how they are doing and then let them share their feelings and emotions. This can be therapeutic and cathartic for the sufferer. People are generally in a place to share because of the depth of the hurt involved. If they do not want to share, that is also their prerogative. It is also appropriate for you as senior leader to suggest the counseling services that your organization provides.

If the professional hardship that your cadre member faces is something you know from your own firsthand experience, you can share your own perceptions of how it could be a positive circumstance and the opportunities that could evolve from it. Depending on how close to the event and the pain involved, the person may or may not be open to such comments. You'll need to apply some emotional intelligence. If the cadre member persists with bitterness deep enough to affect the quality of work and the morale of other team members, and if the person does not respond to your attempts to help, then you face the choices of whether or not this person has a future on the team.

In these types of cases generally, the question routinely comes up about how much time the leader should invest in personal support or other ways of dealing with it. That is of course a judgment call, but senior leaders do need to set aside time for this type of "leadership action." Many managers allow their schedule to be so filled with various activities and responsibilities that they see dealing with a human problem as a waste of valuable time. In terms of pure leadership, dealing with the problem is an excellent use of time.

You can assist your cadre members in the introspection process by advising them about the "Questioning Method." The method says that leaders should always be asking themselves questions such as these:

- Why did I have such a strong positive or negative response to that person, event, or comment? Why did it hit me like it did?
- Why didn't I pay any attention to a certain situation, whereas everyone else involved became really agitated about it?
- Why do I get upset about certain things and ignore or am passive about other very similar items?
- What is it about my boss and superior that I like and what is it that I dislike? What are the reasons for my answers?
- How could I perform a certain leadership or management function well? What would be involved in doing it better?

Individuals can journal their answers to increase self-awareness and improve their long-term effectiveness.

The next chapter moves on to the third "E," education.

Building Leadership Character: Experience

1. What positive leadership behaviors have you developed as a result of your experience? Who, if anyone, helped you make these gains?

2. To what extent does your current organization help you continue to develop through new experience?

3. What further experiences might be most useful in developing your leadership skills and behaviors?

4. How effectively are you and your organization using stretch assignments to develop new leaders? What can you do to improve that?

5. What great leaders' lives might you choose to study in order to learn from their experience?

6. How well is your own cadre of leaders doing in terms of benefiting from experiences? What further support or incentives might be useful?

7. Are there new behaviors you may want to learn for helping junior leaders benefit from hardship?

Chapter Five

Education

In this chapter I use the terms *education* and *training* somewhat interchangeably. Of course, outside either activity, the news media inundate us daily with data and information. But simple exposure to information is the relatively easy part; there is a huge difference between that and the genuine understanding that the word *knowledge* implies. Wisdom is even more rare. As Heraclitus, the fifth-century B.C. Greek philosopher said, "Much learning does not teach understanding."

Education refers to a more systematic imparting of knowledge: the awareness of, familiarity with, and understanding of a range of information, facts, principles, or points of view. In addition to knowledge itself, education implies insight, enlightenment, and an opening of the mind. Then there is the step of actually applying what one learns. Education may involve practice but is often separate from the actual accomplishment of some particular task. As a form of education, training generally implies the gaining of new knowledge in more direct service of mastering some task or skill.

The English philosopher Herbert Spencer (1820–1903) said that the true goal of education is the formation of character. For our purposes, education and training are traditional means to teach the behaviors that correspond with good leadership character. Among other things, training can improve essential skills in decision making, communication, coaching and mentoring, team building, problem solving, and conflict resolution.

Organizations often behave as though any problem can be solved by paying for a bit of training. For example, communication training will improve internal communication, problem-solving training will improve skill levels in solving problems, and so on. But indiscriminate training is not a panacea or single cure for every deficiency in skills. Almost always, a great deal needs to be considered and done to make sure that the training actually meets the need and carries through to practice.

In this chapter I summarize best practices in adult education and outline some more specific leadership character education approaches your organization might take, with behaviors (more than internal thoughts or attitudes) as the focus. Behaviors are the practical focal point of character training for leaders.

Best Practices in Adult Education

The current emphasis in adult and especially executive education is "practical application." Organizational leaders want to know that individuals who attend training will gain skills and understandings that are practical and can be applied. They are interested in return on investment and the cost-benefit ratio. With pressures for increasing profit margins, the days are gone when someone is sent to training simply as a perk. In any event, most leaders do not have the time to go to training that has little value. This is all to the good. Effective practical application depends on *effective* training. In turn, effectiveness depends on our being aware of best practices in teaching. A number of best practices can ensure that leadership behaviors taught in the character development process have a lasting effect.

A Practical, Experiential Process

Leadership character education should be as *practical* as possible and based on as many real-world how-to examples as can be found. Practical training teaches how to behave, do, apply, and put things into practice.

Participation. The best practical training is usually highly participatory, based on discussions in small and large groups, group exercises, experiential activities, questions, and so on, all focused mainly on instilling constructive, positive behaviors. Participatory leadership training means encouraging participants to think and question rather than simply to accept and rehearse: Why is this particular behavior a good one for a leader? In what situations would it not be positive? Can it be overused? Participants need the freedom to raise these questions, and trainers need to be able to explain or guide the group to wise conclusions. Effective questioning is essential because, as Socrates taught, questions force us to think, and, as Martin Luther King Jr. said, "Nothing pains people more than having to think."

Problem Solving. Practical training should focus on solving problems. U.S. World War II hero General George Catlett Marshall said that solving problems is a primary function of leaders. Leaders get paid to get results. Leadership training focuses on behaviors that help someone deal with pressing people problems. This can start with behaviors that enhance communication and managerial courage, improve self-control and caring, and promote optimism.

Direct Experience. Adult training should be as hands-on and as experiential as possible. Adults learn best by doing and by improving through repetitions of doing. As Socrates' philosophical descendant Aristotle remarked, "What we have to do, we learn by doing. We are what we repeatedly do. Excellence then is not an act but a habit." The experiential nature of adult learning means that long lectures tend to be ineffective, but short "lecturettes" can be used to introduce the core principles and foundational ideas needed for the transition into experiencing and practicing behaviors.

Detailed Handouts. Visual materials can complement the verbal aspects of instruction. Handouts of visuals shown during talks and other take-away materials allow participants to review the information after the training. Participants should be informed in advance that handouts will be given out, and the handouts should be detailed enough that the participant need take only minimal notes during the actual presentation. In my experience, excessive note taking inhibits learning because it shifts the focus from absorbing and processing what is being spoken in the moment to writing as quickly as possible. Seldom do lecturers speak at a pace that allows anyone to write notes fast enough to get all the key points. Lecture notes generally are a hodgepodge of incomplete thoughts, ideas, and scribble.

Accommodation for Different Learning Styles. Visuals and handouts are important additions to training in part because they support different learning styles, which is also important in adult education. Another dimension of learning styles involves the diametrically opposed learning styles of introverts and extraverts. Introverts need time and quiet to think and process information. Extraverts, on the other hand, learn best by talking and discussing information. Every class is likely to include both types, and the training approach should accommodate them.

Repetition. Repetition is another essential best practice in adult education. Key principles and behavioral exercises should be presented more than once. No matter how brilliant, people seldom retain a concept by hearing or trying it only once. Because people generally remember only 10 percent of what they hear the first time, it's best to follow the new "Three R's" concept of learning information: review, repeat, and reinforce. Thus information should be gone over more than once, preferably with different examples and perspectives each time. These Three R's provide an effective method to ensure the concepts are well conveyed.

Follow-Up. Effective adult education also requires follow-up experiential activities to reinforce behaviors. These activities should be creative and also challenge the resourcefulness of the participants. Creativity that is encouraged in training will inevitably transfer into innovative behaviors at work.

Debriefing.   Debriefing after training and experiential sessions is another important practice. Debriefings help ensure that key points have been presented and reinforced effectively and that important parts have not been omitted or passed over lightly. The U.S. Army refers to this type of debriefing as an After Action Review (AAR). At its best, an AAR includes as many participants as is practical to invite and accommodate. Because it involves the expression of what might be taken for criticisms and dissatisfactions, efforts should be made to make it safe for everyone involved.

Ongoing Education.   Adult training should be structured as an ongoing process and not simply as an isolated program or event. Process learning is continuous. A program has both a distinct start and end date. A process, on the other hand, has a distinct start date but not an end date.

Advance Materials.   As part of the process approach, read-ahead materials should be sent to participants prior to gathering for training. Such materials are particularly useful for introverts who appreciate more time to process information. Read-ahead items can reduce the length of training sessions and increase the impact when the session actually takes place. Other materials that can be sent to participants prior to the training are the training agenda, the objectives, the approach, logistical instructions, and anything that reduces the participants' anxiety about the upcoming experience.

Process also means that there should be postprogram activities to check on participants' progress. These could include reinforcing key information through the Three R's, follow-on surveys or questionnaires, coaching, accountability mechanisms, readings, and so on. It can also include tasks and projects in which the participant practices something or tries out a certain behavior and then reports back to the group about how it worked or what was learned. Follow-on activities can also involve journaling, reflection, and introspection. Postprogram activities ensure that the behavioral learning continues and is a process, rather than ending when the training session ends.

Personal Assessment.   Finally, assessing one's own behavioral impact can be extremely effective in the adult learning process. This includes individual or 360-degree personality assessment instruments, solicited behavioral feedback, and self-reflection. These are all excellent forms of leadership behavioral impact assessment because they help us to understand the impact of our behavior and also provide insights on what we need to change to be more effective and influential.

The Trainer's Role

Throughout the training process, the adult trainer's role is more that of a facilitator than of an expert or authority who prescribes, directs, or mandates. Facilitation is effective because it reduces defensiveness and push-back, encourages participation, stimulates thinking, promotes retention, and lends itself to more successful application.

Although others can facilitate, your best teachers and trainers are likely to be those who have actually done what is being taught and have themselves successfully led others. This background enhances their credibility and increases their overall impact.

Great leader trainers have a vast repertoire of relevant stories, illustrations, anecdotes, metaphors, analogies, and parables involving the behaviors that are being taught. These are an extremely important resource for adult learning and retention. Abraham Lincoln had a custom of interspersing his conversations with anecdotes, incidents, and witticisms that impressed and entertained his listeners. Theodore Roosevelt and Chester A. Arthur are two other U.S. presidents well known as accomplished raconteurs (Degregario, 1997).

As Lincoln's example suggests, appropriate humor is another effective technique that great leaders and trainers use to promote adult learning. Clever one-liners and lightly making fun of oneself (one of Lincoln's regular practices) usually work best. Too much self-deprecation, lengthy or off-color jokes, shocking language, and ridicule of other people, groups, or political parties should all be avoided. Although listeners may laugh, the net result for the leader is likely to be a loss of credibility and respect. Disparaging humor also creates an unsafe environment for some that inhibits their ability to learn and retain.

One should also generally avoid slang, junk words, clichés, or phrases that tend to appeal to a particular gender, ethnicity, or type of enthusiast.

One unfortunate training philosophy recommends an adversarial relationship between the trainers and participants, claiming that this negative approach actually promotes learning. My own view is that this is not a constructive trainer technique. It may produce some learning, but it also carries many disadvantages. The approach diminishes trust and, as a result, more learning is apt to be lost than transmitted.

Beyond the trainer-trainee relationship, another effective approach is to establish postprogram developmental coaching relationships with the boss, a peer, or a professional coach. A coach can also be an accountability partner (sometimes called a *success partner*). Answering to an accountability partner has proven extremely effective in adult learning follow-through.

Elements of a Character Education Process

It is not the goal of this book to outline—nor is it realistic to expect—one plan or model of leadership character training that will suit all organizations. Groups differ in too many respects for one size to fit all. But beyond best-practice principles for adult education, a number of other suggestions can be offered for how to approach and conduct the process. This section discusses a number of them. Keep in mind that the education "E" is but one of five ways to view and support leadership character development.

A Good Beginning

A good way to begin the process is to conduct an overview briefing with your cadre of leaders. This session should outline what you are thinking—how the initiative is being considered as a developmental process whose goals are positive and preventive, rather than to fix an existing problem. After hearing what this process will or might be like, participants can be asked for their impressions and reactions: Which elements do they think may be effective, which not, and why? Any initiative is more effective if participants commit to it, and this type of discussion helps get their buy-in.

In early discussions, definitions should be compared and contrasted for terms such as *character, ethics, integrity, values, standards,* and *morality.* Another important early topic of discussion is the personal and organizational consequences of being a leader of character (or not). At this stage, relevant examples of leaders, both historical and contemporary, can be presented and discussed to articulate lessons to be learned and applied.

The organization's environment of values and culture (discussed in Chapter Six) can also be examined early in the training, in relation to the actions and behavior that reflect good character. An added advantage of this approach is that it can reveal important insights into the existing culture and whether the company's stated values are still practical, realistic, and current. This is worth detailed discussion. Specific questions might be how the value system actually plays out currently in customer service, product quality, caring for employees, promotion of the organization's mission and vision, and social, environmental, and local community responsibilities.

One opening event for a character development training process could move through the following sequence of activities:

1. Participants each share with the group the biggest ethical challenges they have faced to date and how they handled them.

2. Participants describe the biggest ethical challenges they face in their current positions.

3. The group discusses the current organization's culture and value system and how well it promotes ethical conduct.

4. The group discusses what, if anything, inhibits ethical conduct.

5. Participants share opinions about what could be done to ensure greater ethical conduct within the organizational culture.

Behavioral Goals Based on Leadership Attributes

On a personal level, developing leadership character means increasing positive, constructive leadership behaviors and reducing or eliminating negative ones. This section summarizes a helpful tool for this process—a list of good leadership behaviors that fall under each of the five leadership attributes—courage, caring, optimism, self-control, and communication. Appendix C contains a more detailed version that you can adapt into a rating sheet for yourself and your developing leaders. You can score items from 1 to 5. From this exercise you and your cadre can decide what behaviors should be stopped, started, or changed. You can also make notes on which behavioral strengths you want to ratchet to a higher level.

Results of this type of self- or cross-rating will help you focus the curriculum of leadership character training on what participants see as important learning goals.

Courage

Communicates vision

Accepts risk and responsibility

Acts with courage

Decides with assurance

Delegates and empowers

Perseveres

Addresses conflict

Displays independence and resourcefulness

Stays self-aware and is self-sustaining

Caring

Practices good basic social skills

Hears others

Nurtures and develops others

Recognizes and leverages the talents of others

Treats people fairly and individually

Works well with people of different backgrounds

Monitors personal effect on others and on groups

Deals well with others in times of change

Optimism

Displays a positive attitude and commitment

Challenges negative formulations and assumptions

Looks for possibilities

Inspires optimism

Responds well to setbacks

Stays tuned to the future

Displays self-assurance

Self-Control

Displays long-term patience and endurance

Adapts

Maintains and projects personal calm

Coordinates well with others

Handles own emotions well

Uses own strengths well

Stays in control of self

Deals well with personal stress

Controls appetites and exercises

Communication

Speaks well

Performs well

Writes well

Communicates well nonverbally

Communicates the positive vision of the organization

Listens actively and well

Practices and encourages open communication

Strengthens team communication

Stays aware of multicultural differences

Keeps higher-ups informed

The list will help you keep training focused on specific behaviors rather than just intentions. Use it as you plan specific exercises, discussions, role-plays, case studies, experiential activities, self-assessments, and reflection. The list should also be applicable to the fifth and final "E" (evaluation), presented in Chapter Seven. They can provide a natural link between the character development process and evaluation tools such as 360-degree assessments. These undertakings can be as creative and extensive as you or your cadre members wish to be.

Examining Dilemmas

Psychologist Lawrence Kohlberg (see Chapter One) believed that the discussion of moral dilemmas was a critical element in the process of moral development, at the point that an individual could integrate them into behavioral choices (Kohlberg & Turiel, 1971). At their best, dilemmas force individuals to reflect on their current reasoning processes and deal with any contradictions—a key step in changing, managing, and adjusting their behaviors.

Developmental training in leadership character should include case studies and situations involving ethical dilemmas. These can include scenarios that require the leader to make difficult moral choices and "best-of-the-worst" decisions. Discussions and exercises can consider how the presence or absence of certain leadership behaviors will affect the making of choices. They can also explore potential behavioral pressures on leaders originating from market competition, profit margins, performance expectations, and the organization's culture. The short- and long-term implications of a lapse of leadership character can also be relevant here, and there are many real-world leadership examples to discuss.

The team could discuss stories and studies in which the character of leaders is reflected in their behavior and choices. The discussion can allow your own cadre to examine how they would have handled a situation and why. (Appendix D presents a list of scenarios for discussion, including several dilemmas.)

Contributions from Leaders and Others

As the leader who is initiating the leadership character development process, you can share experiences of how you behaved in different professional dilemmas and what you learned. Few things have more power or impact than firsthand stories, particularly from the boss.

Other senior leaders should also facilitate some of the discussions and provide their thoughts about moral and ethical behaviors and choices, sharing their own experiences in handling ethical dilemmas in the course of their careers. Sharing experiences and revealing influences that formed and reinforced their behavior is a powerful way for senior leaders to engage in dialogue about character with your organization's emerging leaders. Sharing such experiences is highly motivational for senior leaders themselves, lessening the chances that they themselves will lapse in the future, because they will know that junior leaders have them "under the microscope" to see if they practice what they preach. In his seventeen years as CEO of General Electric Jack Welch spoke at GE's Management Development Center (Crotonville) a total of 250 times. Generally these were four-hour sessions in which he shared his ideas with his cadre of leaders and listened to their thoughts and ideas. No doubt this forum is one of the key reasons General Electric experienced few serious ethical scandals during the Welch era.

Not just senior leaders but leaders at all levels of the organization should act as trainers. Bring in junior leaders whose actions have exhibited positive and constructive leadership behaviors supported by courage, caring, optimism, self-control, and so on. Doing this shows support, enhances buy-in, and sets a positive example for the organization's whole leadership cadre. Also, the organization's senior leaders should not just speak or facilitate but also participate as learners in the training. This puts you all on the same page and strengthens your shared frame of reference.

Another resource to bring in is retired leaders from both the public and private sectors to share their experiences, again examining the ethical dilemmas they faced in their careers. Such presentations can generate valuable discussion between the speaker and your cadre. They can lead to productive comparisons and contrasts of how the ethical standards and society have changed in recent times, and the implications of those changes.

Ethical standards vary from one national culture to another. Speakers can be brought in to discuss their own cross-cultural and global experiences, exploring how these differing standards manifest themselves in both interpersonal and business dealings.

Professionals (trainers, consultants, and subject matter experts) can be brought in to do training sessions ranging from ninety minutes to several days on character, behavior, and ethics. This may be especially useful when the team is tackling some particularly stressful challenge.

Of course, you can also send small groups or individual junior leaders for outside formal training courses on the topics of character, ethics, or integrity that are offered by university executive education departments or the various ethical training institutes around the country. Courses on character invariably will touch on behaviors relevant to leadership. When attendees return, they can be asked to provide both a written and verbal report to the cadre on what they learned and the new insights gained. While outside courses should never be the primary means of an organization's leadership character training, they can help individual leaders and can infuse your process with new ideas for improvement.

Some Additional Topics to Cover

In addition to helping junior leaders understand and strengthen their own current attributes and leadership behaviors, several related topics are important to cover. One is the implications for leadership character of an organization's responsibility in the community, society, and broader environment.

Company policies on sensitive issues like equal opportunity, sexual harassment, use of alcohol or drugs in the workplace, workplace violence, and so on should also be reviewed and explored. It's important to reinforce the positive and constructive example that leaders need to set in these regards. Center some discussion on examples of what happened to real but anonymous leaders who violated these policies. Real-life examples are incredibly powerful in encouraging restraint, providing wisdom to the simple, and showing that the company has both the courage and the mechanism to enforce its policies.

Every character development educational process should also take on and emphasize the topic of safety. Full engagement and buy-in will only come from employees who feel safe at work. Consider this real example, which an employee of a manufacturing plant in Michigan shared in one of my classes. To increase production, plant managers ordered the safety guards removed from the processing equipment. When OSHA came for its scheduled inspection, managers had the guards put back on the equipment. When the inspectors left, the safety guards were again ordered removed. You can judge for yourself what worker morale was like at the plant. In addition to general safety of equipment and process, employees also need to feel safe from violence, by outsiders or other employees.

Ongoing Reading and Discussion

In addition to being used in relation to actual training sessions, books and articles on the topics of leadership character, ethics, integrity, and morality can be read and discussed in ongoing conversations you share with your cadre of leaders. Once a month or once a quarter, discussions can be held over breakfast or lunch, or on a Friday afternoon just prior to happy hour. People generally are more open and inclined to converse when food and drink are provided.

A reading club should have a theme. For example, it can focus on leaders of history who were known for great leadership character. Subject matter can include not only books but historical documentary or feature videos and movies about them, as well as visits to museums or historical sites. Follow-on discussions can take off from general opening questions such as these:

- Why was this individual noted for leadership character?
- What were the influences that developed this leadership character?
- What are the major leadership character lessons that can be learned from this individual?
- What were some of the constructive and positive leadership behaviors that this person demonstrated?

Previous chapters have suggested a number of lives to study. McCain's *Character Is Destiny* (2005) previews many more. Here are some others:

Lives Worth Studying

Susan B. Anthony	Organizer for women's right to vote
Clara Barton	Founder of American Red Cross
Jimmy Carter	Humanitarian and statesman
Queen Elizabeth I	Possibly England's greatest ruler
Henry J. Heinz	Industrial innovator
Lewis and Clark	Expedition leaders
James Madison	U.S. president and major force in the creation of basic American law
Thurgood C. Marshall	Civil rights attorney
Ronald Reagan	Conservative emblem and U.S. president
Walter Reuther	Labor organizer
Branch Rickey	The executive who integrated professional baseball
John A. Roebling	Builder of the Brooklyn Bridge
Conrad Adenauer	First president of the Federal Republic of Germany
Mother Teresa	Humanitarian
Margaret Thatcher	Prime minister of Britain
Harry S Truman	U.S. president
Maggie Lena Walker	First woman president of a U.S. bank
John Paul II	Religious leader who contributed to the fall of communism
Ida B. Wells	Human rights author who helped organize the NAACP
Benjamin O. Davis Sr.	Pioneer of military racial integration (first African American general)

Mary Lyon	Transformed women's education; founder of Mount Holyoke College
Hector Garcia	Advocate for Hispanic rights and medical care
Patricia Roberts Harris	First woman to be the dean of the Howard University Law School; first African American woman to be a U.S. ambassador and to serve as a presidential cabinet member
Chief Joseph	Military strategist; leader of the Nez Percé tribe in the late 1800s
Andrew Jackson	Advocate for the common man
George Washington Carver	Botanist and inventor
Robert E. Lee	Advocate for reconciliation after the American Civil War
Jim Bunning	Hall of Fame baseball player and U.S. congressman
Moshe Dayan	Soldier and statesman
Red Auerbach	Author, coach, and sports executive
Dag Hammarskjöld	Diplomat and statesman

The five main attributes discussed in this book (courage, caring, optimism, self-control, and communication) can serve as additional organizing concepts for analyzing these lives. Here are other good questions to ask:

- How clear was their vision of what they wanted to accomplish?
- Were they pursuing a cause greater than themselves?
- Were they principled individuals with a clearly defined personal value system? Were their values conventional for their time?

- How did they respond to hardship or adversity? Always the same? Always well?
- How did they respond to critics and opponents? How did they respond to fame?
- How consistent were they in focus and behavior? Were there low times in their lives? If so, how did they handle them?
- What evidence did they show of caring about other individuals?
- What has been their lasting legacy and reputation?

Self-Education

In addition to creating a formal organizational training process, you can develop leadership character by modeling and supporting continuing self-education. Some individuals are much better at self-education than at playing student in a group. For many very capable leaders, self-education may be the best or even the only way:

- Winston Churchill said that he was always ready to learn but that he did not like being taught.
- Colin Powell was an indifferent student but his parents were great readers and his home was filled with books. While a young man he was constantly reading, which helped create his personal vision.
- Benjamin Franklin left school at the age of ten. Inspired by his work in printing he began a systematic program to educate himself in science, philosophy, and foreign languages. He remains one of the recognized intellectual giants in our nation's history (Brands, 2002).
- Jack London, the best-selling and highest-paid American author of his time, had little formal schooling but was an avid reader, educating himself at public libraries. He eventually attended a university but stayed only six months, finding it not alive enough (Joicey, 2002).

- Madam C. J. Walker, an African American woman born to freed slaves in 1867, never went to school and was totally self-educated. By creating hair products for black women she became one of the first self-made woman millionaires. Her favorite saying was, "I got my start by giving myself a start" (Bundles, 2001).

- Thomas Edison did poorly in school. He was, however, self-taught and totally absorbed in his work. He learned primarily from following his own passion. His inventing was a way of life that focused on hard work, experiential learning, and a singular focus to help mankind. Many times he did not go home at the end of the day but slept on a cot in a side room of his lab (Josephson, 1959).

- The Wright brothers both hated schoolwork. They learned from their own personal study and in their own way. A key lesson came from reading German inventor Otto Lilienthal's writings about gliders.

Do all you can to instill the idea that self-education is an important personal responsibility. When leaders understand this, they show greater motivation, retention, and practical application of what they learn. Your organization can support character self-education by creating, actively maintaining, and promoting the use of an in-house library of leadership books, CDs, DVDs, videotapes, audiotapes, and possibly other resources. Cadre members can also be given an allowance to buy materials online or from a major bookseller. Thomas Carlyle, the renowned English historian (1775–1881), said that the true university in his day was a collection of books, and the same holds true in ours.

Readers are leaders and leaders are readers. When leaders say (as many do) that they don't have time to read, respond by saying they don't have time *not* to read. Well-written biographies are excellent not only because they talk about challenges, behaviors, and ethical dilemmas but also because they can be so absorbing that a reader does not resent the time it takes to read them. Good collections of quotations can also provide a great deal of wisdom in very few words.

Character self-education and support can also be found outside the organization in prayer and other spiritual practices. While you cannot mandate this type of activity, you can certainly encourage it. For example, you can offer voluntary sessions to learn how spiritual activities have changed or enhanced the behaviors of various leaders. Firsthand testimonials are an effective method for this type of training when they allow the cadre to ask questions. An interesting example of constructive spiritual behavior comes out of World War II. In postwar military research, it was established that soldiers who prayed at times requiring courage (moments of danger, decision, or stress) seemed to have greater peace, inner strength, confidence, and willingness to go on (Stoufer, 1949).

Resistance and Incentives

If you anticipate or see that leaders in your cadre are reluctant to participate in leadership character education, you can give them incentives to encourage them to do so. For example, you can offer a pay or bonus incentive, time off, books and subscriptions, or any other perks that are available and reasonable in your organization. Remember that a development process involving leadership character is an investment. If you think this initiative is expensive or awkward, then consider how much an ethical lapse by one of the organization's leaders would cost in terms of time, money, resources, legal fees, and negative publicity.

Remember also that education and training need to mesh with the other four "E's," especially experience. At the end of the day, Roger Schank, educator and founder of Cognitive Arts, is probably right that we don't learn by being told and that for the most part schooling (at least for our purposes) is a waste of time. Learning and schooling, he says, have very little in common. If you want to learn, go out and experience something. Schank promotes apprenticeships and internships for high school students, which he feels are infinitely better learning experiences than the traditional classroom (Zuckerman, 2004). Together with training, try to give increased and varied responsibilities to all members of your leadership cadre.

The next chapter deals with "E" number four—your organization's environment.

Building Leadership Character: Education

1. Looking back on your life, what roles have education and training played in your own character development? What leadership behaviors have they taught you?

2. In what ways is your organization already using best practices in adult education? Who are its in-house experts?

3. What training resources does your organization possess that could support a leadership character training process?

4. What training might you offer in support of stretch assignments?

5. How might you modify the checklist in Appendix B for use with your leadership cadre?

6. Would an ongoing book discussion group be worth forming at your organization? Why or why not?

7. What leadership character self-education do you practice? How might you encourage your cadre in self-education?

Chapter Six

Environment

Environment here refers mainly to the culture of an organization—its society, collective personality, attitudes, customs, traditions, and outlook. The concept of organizational culture carries with it the idea of an identity, a meaningful unity of ideas, achievements, capabilities, and vision. Metaphorically, culture is the air the organization breathes, the water it drinks, and the ground it walks on. The company culture and way of life are shaped and developed over time by the actions and values of its people (Klann, 2003b).

Organizational cultures can and sometimes *must* change. In the 1970s the U.S. Army changed from a conscript force to an all-volunteer force. Overnight the culture changed. The new value system required that leaders take better care of people, treat them with respect and dignity, and remove as many organizational barriers as possible within their level of authority. This was a significant change from the old army culture that valued behaviors that were as directive, prescriptive, and harsh as necessary to get the job done. Many within the system simply could not adjust to this new army and its vastly different value system. They were either miserable or left the service. It was a significant learning experience for me regarding how changing organizational values affect the personal values of leaders, along with their subsequent behavior.

An organization's environment can greatly encourage or impede the development of leadership character. It can support and promote positive and influential behaviors—or not. At the heart is the system of values that the culture truly reflects, and with which you and other leaders in the company are trying to behave consistently and in concert.

This chapter looks mainly at organizational values, how they may focus or conflict, and your role in defining and promoting good leadership values. It also discusses positive and negative environmental characteristics, and the centrality of good communication. Finally it talks about building character development into your company's business plan.

The Driving Force of Values

Values identify what is most important to an organization and its culture—its core principles, convictions, and priorities. Every organization and every person within it has a value system. Organizational value systems lend focus. Along with the personal values of the organization's leaders, such systems drive leaders' behaviors and choices and affect a leader's ability to have a positive influence on others. Ideally, a company's value system positively directs, guides, and supports your own sound leadership behaviors and those of your leadership cadre. If the organization's value set emphasizes positive leadership behaviors, it can provide benchmarks for leadership character development and help keep leaders within appropriate ethical and moral boundaries.

Written and Unwritten Values

Most organizations have a formal, written system of values that appears on framed wall posters, wallet cards, corporate Web sites, and the like. Usually it mentions the importance to the organization of customer service, quality, productivity, ethical conduct, employee safety, support of diversity, environmental awareness, community relations, and so on. These values vary somewhat based on the industry, product, or service provided.

But culture is like the air around us; it is everywhere in an organization. So unwritten values also evolve in every company culture.

These unwritten norms can be strongly felt within an organization and greatly shape the culture. Unwritten values develop over time and eventually become part of the company's customs and traditions, including rules and expectations about behavior. For example, unwritten rules may abound about whether or not a leader can circumvent the hierarchical chain of command, about what one must do to get promoted or avoid getting fired, or how much social participation is expected of a leader. Discerning these unpublished values requires some emotional intelligence on the part of junior leaders, and doing so can be as important as excellent performance (and at times perhaps more important).

For effective leadership character development, all leaders need a clear understanding of their corporate culture, both written and unwritten. This is essential because knowing the company values in both arenas is what makes it possible to behave consistently with them.

Murky or Conflicting Values

From the environment you as leader and your leadership cadre need to learn the behaviors that are acceptable or expected, and those that are not. Inevitably, you make many choices and decisions based on the values and expectations of the organization. Of course, this depends on your understanding those requirements and on their being consistent among themselves.

Unfortunately, comprehending the company's value system is not always an easy task, and many times what is said in the written values statement is not the bottom line. Some things may appear in the values statement because they are politically correct or because leadership has an unfulfilled wish they were true. There may also be key unwritten values that become increasingly significant the longer one is part of the organization. You need to bring your own emotional intelligence into play in helping junior leaders navigate these problems.

While organizations evolve patterns of behavior that are endorsed, encouraged, expected, and compensated in both leaders and employees, such patterns are not necessarily good. If the behavior patterns are positive and promote the general welfare, then chances are the organization can implement an effective development process for leadership character. However, when positive patterns of behavior are not emphasized over negative ones, the message is clear: the organization values and prefers qualities other than character and thus has little interest in character development.

For example, an almost mandatory value of a for-profit organization is high profit margins and ever-increasing earnings. This value may be such a powerful driving force that it causes the organization to do things that conflict with other written values and with the personal values of midlevel leaders, lower-level leaders, and employees in general: mistreating, exploiting, or neglecting employees; taking shortcuts on safety; looking away from abuses to the environment; ignoring community responsibilities; misrepresenting information to the news media; taking advantage of suppliers; using second-rate materials; or being dishonest with customers.

In most companies, a senior leader has considerable power to curb or reduce these tendencies, in light of the fact that most of them turn out to be counterproductive in the long run. But it is possible to find oneself in what amounts to a toxic culture. Near the end of the chapter I will discuss what options you may have.

Your Role in Establishing and Endorsing Values

Within an organizational culture, senior leaders can use their own vision, values, and standards to establish the boundaries of conduct and other expectations placed upon their cadre. Leaders at all levels need to work together to establish an environment that is open to the character development of leaders. Having a set of clear, written, detailed, and practical organizational values (as opposed to a wish list) can help to create such an atmosphere. The values must be feasible and realistic rather than idealistic nonsense, so that senior leaders can ensure that the leadership cadre and other employees live and behave according to those values rather than make empty gestures. In addition, of course, senior leaders must themselves model the values.

Relevant, realistic values are more likely to be accepted and followed if they embody the input of all levels of the organization. Values simply declared and mandated by senior leaders to the rest of the organization will receive less buy-in and ownership.

A value set that emphasizes positive leadership behaviors and influential traits can serve as an important benchmark for developing leadership character. Such a value set can also help you and other leaders stay within the ethical and moral boundaries of the organization—provided there are clearly understood and enforced disciplinary consequences for violations at all levels of the organization. *At all levels* is the key phrase here, because the actions and attitudes of you and other senior leaders will set the tone and standard for the organization regardless of any other written or unwritten policies or values. It will always be up to you to model and pass down the finer points of organizational environment, culture, and values. You can teach and show what is more important, what less; which consistent patterns of behavior and choices are appropriate and which are not. You can train junior leaders to behave and exercise positive influence in concert with the organization's values, based on your knowledge of how things really work, including the politics involved. You can help your cadre recognize the unwritten protocols and conventions of the organization and how they should shape a leader's behavior. You can teach how decisions are made and problems get solved; how one gets recognized, rewarded, and promoted; and how one can avoid the pitfalls. Knowing these things is extremely important for your leadership cadre because to succeed in any given culture, they must learn how to work and behave within the norms and values that drive the system.

As Chapter Three implied, by working closely with your cadre of leaders, you can establish a powerful bond that will result in their emulating all your positive (and perhaps even negative) behaviors. The best mentoring relationships arise from the bonding that occurs in subordinate-superior relationships. In that context they flow out naturally, without seeming forced, assigned, or programmed. Most often, your values will become your leadership cadre's values, regardless of what is written in the organizational values statement.

Environments Conducive to a Successful Character Development Initiative

Some organizational cultures provide more fertile ground than others for a character development initiative. Important factors include functional homogeneity, the presence of committed leaders with a willingness to accept some risk, a genuine vision, and a culture that truly values people.

Functional Homogeneity

The organization should be relatively homogeneous in function. Homogeneity results in a strong corporate identity and uniform values and goals. Agreement on priorities provides a basis for development. The more similar in function the business units are, the easier it will be to reach consensus on the priorities and focus of a developmental initiative. An organization can develop people to work in its own environmental culture, but not in others (McCall, Lombardo, & Morrison, 1988). Optimally, the parent organization has business units that support the same or similar products. For example, one business unit makes tractors, another bulldozers, and a third backhoes. Such similar missions facilitate leadership development assignments that involve taking on job appointments and sharing responsibilities and functions across business boundaries. This is much more difficult if one business unit makes train engines, another light fixtures, and a third home appliances.

The Presence and Influence of Leaders Like You

Leaders like yourself are the next most important ingredient for the success of a leadership character development initiative. Leadership character development programs are visionary and avant-garde, and therefore do entail risk. Undertaking one implies that you and your other senior leaders see value in accepting risk; you understand the tremendous return on the investment of such a process in relation to general employee development and to serious succession planning. It implies you recognize the value of influential behavior and therefore support its learning. To consider such an initiative takes a high degree of courage, creativity, and commitment of resources, along with a strong belief in humanity. It also requires that your own values in these respects be reasonably consistent with your surrounding organizational culture and environment. If they are not, your process will probably not receive real organizational support and endorsement.

If leadership character development is a priority, then you and the organization's other leaders must make that clear, constantly placing an emphasis on it and making sure it permeates the culture. This significantly increases the probability it will be taken seriously and sustained. Concrete actions need to demonstrate that it isn't just another "flavor of the month." Actions need to include the allocation of reasonable amounts of time, effort, and other resources to the process. While making sure that the leadership character development process does not become burdensome, you must also make sure that it isn't seen as optional, a nice thing to do—that is, as an activity that can fall by the wayside every time business slows. If that attitude takes root, the initiative most likely will not survive.

The average manager, administrator, and bureaucrat will never seriously consider a character development initiative. In fact, many average-to-mediocre managers resist any developmental effort at all because they don't want to divert the time, money, effort, and resources away from the primary mission. They don't see the need; they fear losing their own best people, or they simply won't take the risk. In every profession or business, there are relatively few real leaders, much less exceptional ones (McCall, Lombardo, & Morrison, 1988).

An Indispensable Vision

As was already briefly pointed out, creating a leadership development initiative does require vision. It takes the commitment of someone who constantly looks for how the company could grow, change, and evolve for the better. It takes a leader who not only can envision success but can communicate that vision and follow through with skill and drive. Such people exist. Consider Walt Disney, who died before Disney World in Orlando was completed. Months after his death, when the opening ceremony was concluded, an admirer of Walt's said to Mrs. Disney, "It's too bad Walt didn't get to see this!" Mrs. Disney replied about her visionary husband, "Oh, but he did! He certainly did see it!" She of course was saying that Walt had seen it as a vision.

H. Smith Richardson Sr. was another extraordinary visionary whose innovative ideas on succession planning and developing leaders made the Center for Creative Leadership a reality. As he said, "It takes boldness to invest in programs of uncertain potentialities, but it is out of such initiatives that some of the greatest discoveries have been made."

A Culture That Values Its People

Finally, your organization's culture must absolutely value its people, and in particular its leadership capital. Many businesses boldly announce that their most important resources are their employees. However, the statement turns into a joke among employees whose company treats them as just another commodity. Many companies give little or no consideration to the absolute fact that employees have huge untapped productivity and performance potential. In these cultures, human potential is generally poorly understood, managed, applied, or developed. Many organizational policies actually inhibit human potential with numerous unwitting barriers and job dissatisfiers.

If the company is serious about valuing employees as its most important resource, the obvious next step is to see that they are properly developed, including aspects of character. In other words, the company's leaders should create a company culture and value system that supports a viable, long-term leadership character development process. That system needs to be based on the following policies and actions:

- A commitment to the value of people, seeing them as a valuable corporate resource and the key to the organization's future. This includes a vision of how character development can help them fulfill their promise and potential. This requires substantial management actions that demonstrate real care for people. At a minimum, these would include

  A managed succession planning program

  An established early identification method of high-potential performers

  A defined leadership development process

  The creation of stretch job assignments

  Exposure to a variety of effective bosses

- An appreciation for and support of individual learning as a key element of development. Learning should focus on giving your cadre of leaders an understanding of the corporate cultural environment—both its formal value system and its prescribed and expected patterns of behavior. Learning should also include training in support of appropriate patterns of behavior.

- Steps to prevent ethical violations and scandals before they happen. Consistently positive influential behaviors must be part of that prevention.

- Innovation, creativity, and a willingness to try new ideas.

- Comfort with taking risks.

- Willingness to invest resources in projects that will provide long-term and not necessarily short-term returns.

This package of qualities is not particularly common, which is why character development programs are also not at all common. But as society continues to change and leaders are faced with greater ethical challenges, more and more character development programs will appear.

Responding to a Toxic Culture

Earlier in the chapter, I described a type of corporate culture that undermines leadership character development. What if you enter an organization that has such a toxic culture? What if the culture of your current organization changes for the worse because of a change in senior leadership or a hostile takeover? What if, because of an extended period of average or mediocre performance, the board of directors mandates certain policies that you regard as ethically questionable to a degree that you are not prepared to live with? How will any initiative to develop leadership character play out in such an environment?

Every choice or decision relies on a leader's personal value system in the context of the organization's value system. All is well for both parties if these two value systems are compatible. The challenge comes when they are contradictory or inconsistent. Conflicts and contradiction between organizational and personal values often relate to the following issues:

How downsizing was or is being managed

Having a change made to a key process which you intuitively know, based on your past experience, will fail miserably

Working for managers who are inconsistent in behavior, marginally competent, relationally challenged, or offer very little that can be respected

Being expected to participate in organizational activities that you see as insincere, manipulative, patronizing, condescending, or even exploitive

Being asked to do something that you believe is immoral, illegal, or dishonorable

Seeing your organizational benefits erode and then listening to your senior managers tell you how well the organization is doing and praise the great organizational benefit package

Seeing top performers and those highly qualified passed over for promotion in favor of those who are politically adept or

politically correct, or who have some close relationship to
senior management

For the leader whose value system is in conflict with the organization's values, life isn't easy, and hard choices may be inevitable.
But at least there are choices.

As a leader, you can aggressively try to change the system or policy with which you disagree. In this effort you can use all your powers of persuasion, personal credibility, communication skills, personal
and expert power, and ability to influence. You can be the crusader
for the change. Before you do this, possibly pulling your own leadership cadre into the struggle, evaluate the chances of success. Consider where the policy came from, the personality or personalities
involved, and how open the culture is to reversing established policies and decisions. You and your cadre will also need to consider the
ramifications for your careers. No one benefits from a reputation of
always taking up lost causes, falling on the sword for everything,
or always taking the injured puppy home.

Another option is to be passive and simply live with the contradiction. Perhaps you and your individual cadre members can
adapt and embrace the organization's value system. You may be accused of compromising your values, not having the courage to
change the process, or promoting what you don't agree with through
your silence, but sometimes discretion is the better part of valor.
This is a choice, and each choice entails consequences and trade-
offs. The principle here is that you must decide the degree to which
you will make the organizational values your own.

You can also choose to work around the problem, doing what is
possible within the limitations of the situation. This may not be op-
timal and it may entail quite a lot of frustration, but at least you and
members of your cadre who are of the same mind will feel that
something is being done.

The last choice is to leave the organization and find a position
with another company that is more compatible with your personal
value system. On the surface this may seem like the best option, but

really it is the option of last resort. No organization is perfect, because flawed individuals run them all.

Communication and Other Positive Organizational Attributes

The same five attributes that underlie good leadership character—courage, caring, optimism, self-control, and communication—can also be seen as important basic attributes of an organization's culture. Each can be promoted and encouraged by the culture, its leaders, and a character development process for leaders. For example, Howard Shultz, the chairman of Starbucks, was motivated by his own experience to create a cultural environment of caring at Starbucks. Remembering the strain that not having health benefits placed on his parents, Shultz has given strong evidence of compassion and concern for Starbucks employees, particularly in the form of quality medical benefits (Meyers, 2005). At Microsoft, Bill Gates has created an environment of courageous risk taking and optimistic innovation (Schultz, 2005).

Shelly Lazarus, chairman and CEO of Ogilvy & Mather Worldwide, has created an organizational culture that promotes self-control through the concept of work-life balance. She says that balance is achieved through a host of individual dance steps, from being willing to suffer a little chaos in one's home life to insisting that performance be measured by results, not just time spent on the job. She promotes the notion with her employees that unless you love your work, you won't find balance (Lazarus, 2005).

The fifth attribute, communication, is so essential to a character-developing culture that it deserves some expanded discussion. In an organizational environment, communication should constantly reinforce the values of the organization. From the company executive team down to the minimum-wage hourly worker, everyone must understand the values. Communicating values is an ongoing mission, through actions as well as words.

Communication should spread the word that character is an important consideration in the company's leadership selection choices. Employees should be aware of the criteria and personal qualifications for selection into any high-potential, fast-track program. Those criteria and qualifications are likely to include such things as a proven track record of results, evidence of hard work, solid communication skills, willingness to learn and grow, and a loyal and supportive team spirit. The organization should also communicate how success is gauged for those already in a fast-track program, the things to do and not to do to avoid derailment, and ethical standards of conduct. The latter could begin with all leaders' clear avoidance of improprieties such as any form of discrimination, sexual harassment, illegal drug use, physical violence at the workplace, personal use of company property and resources, or misappropriation of funds.

Some organizational values statements communicate specific behaviors that are seen as reflecting positive character and that enhance success in the organization. These often include initiative, diligence, decisiveness, courage, courtesy, caring, optimism, self-control, and commitment. This type of statement is good because it gives every employee the chance to focus on behaviors that maximize success.

Leaders of your organization should constantly promote open and honest communication. The company culture should support a "positive feedback" environment, including welcoming verbal behavioral feedback and assessment feedback from individual personality assessments like the Myers-Briggs Type Indicator and from 360-degree assessments in which the individual is rated by the boss, peers, direct reports, superiors, and so forth. Without behavioral feedback, no character development process is likely to succeed.

The culture should also embody and communicate a wise policy regarding mistakes. Virtually all organizations have a reward and recognition system, but few have a "mistake system" that handles serious errors effectively and consistently across the institution.

Here I am talking about honest mistakes, not those resulting from laziness, a negative attitude, dishonesty, or general hostility.

Not openly communicating the company position on mistakes and failures can have several negative effects. It can subject leaders to constant negative tension and perpetuate false impressions, which can lead to more and greater mistakes. Lack of open communication can also spawn rumors regarding what will happen to you if you make a big mistake, what may happen if you dare to take risks, and even result in cover-ups and the shifting of blame.

What happens to a capable member of your leadership cadre who makes a doozy of a mistake or fails miserably in a project? In some organizations, one mistake means a leader's career is over. That was common practice in the "Zero Defects" U.S. Army in which I served in the 1970s and 1980s. Some severe cases may merit demotion, probation, exile to a dead-end job, being made a public example, or simply receiving a bad performance review. But you know you have good leaders out there whose mistakes or periodic failures stem from the fact that they are doing things and taking appropriate risks. This is the entire subject of John C. Maxwell's valuable book *Failing Forward: Turning Mistakes into Stepping Stones for Success* (2000).

General Colin Powell tells leaders that they should accept the honest mistakes of their subordinates rather than simply set penalties for them (Duffy, 2005). Mistakes need to be part of a learning process. Once a mistake has been made, the main questions should be what the leader and organization can learn from the mistake and what has been or can be done to recover from the damage. Such learning can be the first step to greatness.

An organization that is sincerely interested in development will be tolerant and focused on the learning, and provide a second chance. Recovery could include extensive developmental feedback, more coaching, and possibly even additional training before being given another chance. Offering a second chance may be a visionary act. It can be highly cost-effective and productive, in view of the often enormous cost of a failed leader to the organization.

Leader Development in the Business Plan

If your organization truly wants to create an environment that develops its employees and generates positive leadership character, that fact should be made evident and concrete in the business strategy and plan. A business plan shows most clearly what the organization values, with more or less detail for any given area of focus.

Inclusion in the business plan confirms to all that character development deserves serious attention and resources. As an advocate for leadership character development, you might write and champion this portion of the strategy. In format, it could look something like Integrated Plan for Developing Leadership Character found in Appendix E. Here are some things that the character development portion might include:

- How much and what type of resources will be allocated for this area: money, materials, infrastructure, personnel (external trainers, consultants, or coaches), time allocation, and so on.

- An integrated plan that covers the character development responsibilities of the organization's leaders at various levels, human resources, the information technology (IT) department, and the training department.

- Who will be the lead individual and the champion of the program, who is held accountable for what, and what the measurement criteria are. The key to success is your support and participation and that of the other senior leaders within the organization. Projects led by line managers have a much higher probability of success than initiatives that come solely through human resources or the training department.

- Learning resources available for the character development process: training; courses; educational center materials such as books, CDs, or DVDs; internal and external trainers and coaches; and interested, accessible, and involved organizational leaders.

- The process and criteria for identifying and selecting high-potential leaders for special assignments.

- Expected outcomes, including measures to prevent and reduce ethical violations and organizational scandals, and resource expenditures for both. Expected outcomes can also include the harmonious and professional behaviors by which the organization will operate.

If any of these details are not included in the business plan, the plan should say where they can be found.

Looking after your organization's culture can play an important part in fostering strong leadership character. The next chapter explores the impact of evaluation, the fifth and final "E."

Building Leadership Character: Environment

1. What main written and unwritten values govern your organization?

2. What roles do you and other leaders currently take in examining, communicating, and endorsing values?

3. How positive is your organizational environment with regard to supporting good leader behaviors, including courage, caring, optimism, self-control, and communication?

4. How well does your organization communicate regarding expectations for leaders and opportunities for developing leaders? How does it treat mistakes?

5. What can you do to make the environment friendlier and more conducive to the character development of leaders?

Chapter Seven

Evaluation

To *evaluate* means to accurately determine the value, worth, content, or status of something. In the context of character development, evaluation involves observing the behavior of members of your cadre, then comparing what they do with the organization's values and standards. The purpose is to identify behavioral strengths and weaknesses and then expand the former while reducing the latter.

Evaluation helps you apply ideas from the other "E's," such as stretch assignments (experience) and training processes (education), more effectively. Together with feedback, evaluation also assists cadre leaders in adjusting their own behaviors for more positive influence. Receiving accurate feedback on behaviors involving character is extremely important for leadership success. Insightful feedback opens leaders' eyes to blind spots and gives them valuable and new perspectives on the impact of their behavior. How can they (or you) know the impact of their own behaviors without being periodically assessed?

Feedback should include information about the appropriateness, quality, consistency, and extent of impact of a leader's behaviors. The feedback can be verbal or written, or can be delivered in the form of a performance appraisal process.

This chapter addresses three different processes for evaluation: behavioral feedback, performance appraisals, and employee discipline. For each, it offers some practical guidelines. First, however, it is worth considering that of the Five E's in a leadership character development process, evaluation is the biggest challenge.

The Challenge of Evaluation

For leaders who initiate a character development process the evaluation "E" is, indeed, the most challenging. All three of its main elements (behavioral feedback, performance appraisals, and discipline) can be difficult to perform and may involve controversial actions. Even the most experienced leader may be challenged by the tasks of giving developmental feedback, presenting a less-than-flattering performance appraisal, or imposing discipline. If any of these steps are not done well, the result can be more and larger problems than the original focus of the feedback, appraisal, or discipline. But if well carried out, these three can greatly benefit the recipient and further enhance the behaviors of the leadership cadre in general.

One way to prepare yourself for evaluating others is to review your own personal resources in terms of the five leadership attributes—courage, caring, optimism, self-control, and communication. If you yourself are well prepared in and able to apply all five, you will be in a position to use evaluation effectively.

First, it takes courage to evaluate well. Because of a lack of courage some leaders never give developmental feedback or write anything but glowing performance appraisals, and they ignore behaviors that might require discipline.

Leaders must also sincerely care about their cadre and their development in order to evaluate well. Behavioral feedback, performance appraisals, and discipline all take time, effort, concentration, and insightful thought. Not to care is either not to do appraisals or to do them in a cursory manner. But if you care enough to show sincere interest and genuine concern, and then to evaluate conscientiously, your cadre will certainly recognize that fact and reciprocate with positive behaviors. The circle strengthens itself. The relationship you develop from both sides through caring evaluation will raise not only the quality of feedback, performance appraisal, and discipline you can give but also the way it is received. Remember that feedback is a gift for which thanks are due.

The attribute of optimism is also relevant here because an optimistic leader is able to present feedback, either positive or developmental, in a way that motivates, supports, and inspires hope. The leader's optimism will generally motivate the junior leaders to accept the behavioral feedback and actually do something with it in practice. The leader's optimism can be key in ensuring that the feedback leads to change in behaviors. A leader whose manner is clinical or casual when delivering feedback, or who puts the entire responsibility of embracing and using the feedback on the recipient, will have much less of a positive impact.

Self-control is important because the leader must remain calm, collected, and under control in sessions involving feedback, performance appraisal, and discipline. There is always the outside chance the recipient will regard it as inaccurate, unjust, or unwarranted and respond with hostility or other strong emotions. When that happens, you as the leader need to remain calm, focused, and self-possessed. Such behavior sets a positive example for the other person, defuses rather than escalates the situation, and enhances the respect and esteem in which you are likely to be held. Few things guarantee the total loss of respect for leaders more than seeing them lose control of themselves.

Finally, situations involving feedback, performance evaluation, and discipline can have much more impact and better effect if the leader in charge has strong communication skills. Whether spoken or in writing, behavioral information will have the most impact if it is presented with finesse, simplicity, clarity, and care. In the wisdom of the American South, you can say just about anything to anyone as long as you preface it with "Well, bless your heart . . .": "Well, bless your heart, aren't you putting on weight!" Well-chosen words can motivate, ease, encourage, and heal. Unadorned bluntness is more likely to demotivate, upset, discourage, and injure.

In evaluation settings, a leader's written, spoken, and nonverbal communication should be well planned and rehearsed, and delivered with professionalism and care. This can make all the difference in how your message is received and whether or not the individual will act on your advice.

Behavioral Feedback

Ongoing feedback is the foundation and core of any developmental experience, and character development is no exception. Without feedback, it is almost impossible for leaders to develop and improve their behaviors. Successful and effective leaders routinely indicate that they have sought *candid behavioral feedback* from their most critical stakeholders—and then acted on it. These stakeholders could include the boss, other superiors, peers, direct reports, customers, clients, suppliers, family members, government regulators, community officials, and the like.

For leadership character development, the purpose of feedback is to start a cycle of opportunity by making your leadership cadre aware of their behavioral influence and impact. Your information lets leaders know how their character is measuring up and how they are progressing toward their character development goals. With this learning and awareness they will be able to adjust their conduct to improve their performance and overall behavioral effectiveness. Most employees, and especially leaders, want feedback in order to know where they stand on issues of character and how they are doing professionally. This is not only a valid desire but also a just employee entitlement. Getting feedback should be part of every organization's value system and employee bill of rights.

Behavioral feedback is essential because all leaders are biased toward the correctness of their behavior and take a certain amount of pride in what they do. Assessment feedback will help clarify that notion and provide information that will help the recipient adjust behavior to be more consistent, influential, and effective.

Giving behavioral feedback develops character in a number of ways. First, behavioral feedback exposes blind spots. It identifies areas of development as well as areas of personal and professional strength. It lets people know whether their behavior is consistent or inconsistent. It also informs them about how much influence and impact their leadership behaviors have. Behavioral feedback will tell your leadership cadre how authentic, sincere, real, and genuine they are perceived to be. Behavioral feedback also shows recipients they are cared about and that their development is considered important. For most cadre members, this is highly motivational. It encourages them to behave in a manner that is even more consistent with your expectations and those of the organization. All this provides a solid foundation for your working with them on character development.

For feedback to be effective, you as a senior leader first need to establish and communicate clear expectations regarding appropriate and effective patterns of behavior. Expectations lay out a road map for behavioral development. En route, you and your junior leaders should stop for periodic feedback sessions to gauge each one's behavioral progress, review the challenges involved in positive behaviors, and look back at how they fared in specific instances when their behavior was tested.

Assessment feedback for character development can focus on behavioral choices that inherently have character implications. Appendix B lists many of these types of behavior. Many relate to decision making, problem solving, conflict resolution, team building, use of funds and other resources, and how people are handled. For example, do a leader's decisions focus primarily on the good of the organization or on personal gain or advantage? Do you and your cadre use and manipulate your employees, or do you choose to treat them with respect, trust, and dignity? Do you always choose to use organizational funds and resources so there would never be any accusations of fraud, waste, and abuse? These are choices on which behavioral feedback is needed to avoid even a hint of impropriety.

Positive and Negative Feedback

Whether positive or negative, behavioral feedback shows recipients they are cared about and that their development is considered important.

Interestingly, many leaders seek behavioral feedback only regarding the negative side—their developmental needs. That is unwise—after all, it was their strengths, not their weaknesses, that got them where they are today, and it is always easier to improve on strengths than it is to eliminate weaknesses. Many times, improving on strengths can neutralize weaknesses. This idea may seem to be in conflict with the notion that a behavioral strength, if overdeveloped or relied upon, can become a liability. But there is no inconsistency here. Almost every junior leader's behavioral strength will need to improve and improve again in the course of promotion to midlevels and senior levels of management. In effect, to prevent *any* behavior from becoming a liability it must be aggressively, continuously upgraded and improved. Behaviors representing strengths should be further developed just like those representing weaknesses.

Another oddity is that, while leaders often prefer feedback on their weaknesses, a negative connotation generally attaches to behavioral feedback. For example, what is the first thing you think of when someone says to you, "I'd like to give you some feedback"? This pattern exists because, traditionally, feedback has been given primarily for negative behaviors or when there is a performance problem. Seldom is it given about ongoing positive or preventive behaviors. Ongoing, balanced positive and negative assessment feedback goes lacking for several reasons: time constraints, apprehension about the recipient's response, the confrontational nature and inherent tension of giving developmental behavioral feedback, and the ever-present possibility of litigation. Negative feedback also goes lacking because people by nature want to be liked. Because negative feedback often elicits a less-than-positive response, many very successful leaders would rather hug the bad deal and tolerate the situation than deliver feedback that might cause things to deteriorate further.

Another main reason for the lack of ongoing, balanced feedback is lack of skill at giving feedback. Giving feedback *is* a skill and does not come naturally to most leaders. It must be learned and constantly practiced. This is something few leaders have the time or desire to do. But this skill is essential for effective character development.

In my view, there is really no such thing as negative behavioral feedback. Even if the feedback criticizes the leader, if it helps keep that leader from career derailment then it is still positive and not negative feedback. As Craig Newmark, the founder of Craigslist, has said about negative feedback, "When someone points out a mistake to you, deal with it—don't go into denial" (Newmark, 2005).

Best Practices in Behavioral Feedback

The starting point for giving good feedback is observing the behaviors of your cadre of leaders as consciously and as sensitively as you can. How can you give valuable assessment feedback to your cadre of leaders if you don't make a concentrated effort to observe their behavior? Your ability to do this is a function of your own emotional intelligence and your own command and recognition of social skills. These prepare you to notice junior leaders' skills and behaviors in observation, discernment, and timing of communication, as well as their diplomatic and political skills and their ways of influencing and developing others below them.

Given your competence at observation, you can go on to exercise a number of vital best practices in giving behavioral feedback for a character development process. Key ideas include having a model; making feedback ongoing, safe, and balanced; and attuning feedback to individuals. The following section expands on each idea. The section after that gives guidelines for conducting a session.

Models and Other Key Practices. One best practice is to follow an effective and proven model for the content of behavioral feedback. Among the best models for feedback is the Center for Creative Leadership's "SBI model" (for situation, behavior, and impact). The SBI model is effective because it reduces the anxiety of the feedback giver and reduces the defensiveness of the feedback receiver. It does not judge, evaluate, or condemn the motives behind the behavior. It simply reports on the behavior in specific terms, as follows:

- S = Situation. What were the specific time, place, and circumstance in which the behavior took place?

- B = Behavior. Behaviors can include observable actions, verbal comments, nonverbal signals, written messages, and personal mannerisms. What specific behavior was noted? The more specifically a behavior is identified, the more likely the recipient is to understand and act on the feedback. Generalities or vague comments are virtually worthless as behavioral feedback.

- I = Impact. Impact refers to the consequences of the behavior: the impact the behavior had on others; what those affected might think, feel, or do as a result of the behavior; and whether the behavior was effective or ineffective.

A second best practice is to make assessment feedback an ongoing process, not just one annual event as part of a performance appraisal. Ongoing feedback has several advantages. Feedback that is given promptly, that is, shortly after the behavior takes place, has a higher impact, in part because the information is fresh (Buron & McDonald-Mann, 1999). Timely feedback can be more specific, allows assessment of usual, simple behaviors, and requires less formality. This type of feedback is the most useful, being more likely to lead to action than feedback postponed for a quarterly or yearly meeting. Also, giving ongoing feedback produces less tension than massing feedback information for delivery at a later date.

Also ongoing should be your efforts to see that feedback is given and received in a *safe environment*—a time and place where a recipient can be open to listening, learning, and applying the information received. Give some thought to when and where you choose to give feedback. Settings might include a neutral area such as a conference room, the junior leader's office, or over breakfast or lunch. People are always more open, agreeable, and amiable over food and drink. Unless the feedback is extremely positive, always avoid delivering it in public. Receiving negative behavioral feedback in public can be demeaning, humiliating, and degrading. Giving someone negative feedback in public is an excellent way to forever lose the respect of the person receiving the feedback. The receiver seldom forgives the leader who does that, or forgets the incident.

If the feedback is about negative behaviors, the session should be scheduled, private, focused, structured, and scripted. Its main points should also be recorded in writing for later reference by the writer. Each of these considerations helps the cadre member to retain personal dignity and makes you more likely to achieve your desired result. The written record and script can also be valuable if there is any fallout from the meeting. Another best practice is weighting ongoing behavioral feedback with more positive than negative comments. In ten years of working in Western Europe I noted cultures where a belief prevailed that developmental feedback was valuable only if it was solidly negative. In my experience, a good ratio for behavioral feedback is about four positives for every negative developmental point. This ratio helps the receiver take both the positive and developmental feedback to heart. All-positive feedback will be dismissed and all-negative will create ill will and resentment.

Finally, as you plan and deliver feedback, stay deliberately aware of your own personal assumptions, prejudices, and biases. Your behavioral feedback says as much about you as it does about the cadre member receiving it. On each occasion, try to step back and ask yourself how your own worldview, emotional economy, or behavioral grid is influencing what you say.

Other writings expand on these and other principles for giving and receiving behavioral feedback. For example, see *Ongoing Feedback: How to Get It, How to Use It* (Kirkland & Manoogian, 1998). Ultimately, the key is to work toward an ongoing consistency in how feedback is solicited, given, received, and acted on.

Best Practices in Feedback Sessions. Some best practices come into play mainly during an actual feedback session.

Prepare for a session by considering who this member of your leadership cadre is as a unique human being and, accordingly, how you should treat this individual. Not everyone reacts to a given style of feedback in the same way. Each will process feedback differently. Extraverts, who talk to think, will generally talk excessively and will probably interrupt several times during the session. Introverts, who always think prior to talking, will probably say very little during the session. They need time to process the information, which you can accommodate by allowing silence during the meeting or by arranging a follow-on meeting at which they can actively respond by sharing their thoughts. Overall, the uniqueness of individuals means that feedback sessions often take surprising turns. Since this is to be expected, you need not allow the fact to intimidate or discourage you or restrict your actions. As I noted earlier, effective evaluation requires courage on both sides of the table. That's especially true during feedback.

As you proceed through feedback sessions, never assume that leaders receiving feedback from you are aware of the impact of their behavior, either positive or negative. Assume that they are not aware of the impact. Even when they have some awareness, it is generally not complete or particularly accurate.

Throughout the session focus behavioral feedback on the impact of the behavior and never on the personality. This is extremely important. Avoid negative judgments on the cadre member's personality or moods. Stick to the impact of the behavior, not the person's reasons for behaving that way. You are not Dr. Phil, Oprah, or Montel. To focus on motives or personality is to raise defenses, reducing the recipient's ability to listen and think rationally. Focusing on personality lays the foundation for long-term problems with a cadre member.

Best practice advice also includes a number of ideas about tone and choice of language. To begin, your tone of voice matters greatly. You communicate more with your tone of voice than with the actual words. Your tone gives more real indication than your words do of what you are feeling and thinking. Of course, I don't mean to imply that your choice of words is not important. Both are worth practice and careful attention.

Avoid embellished, exaggerated, or categorical statements about the cadre member's behavior, such as "you never" or "you always." Seldom do people "always" or even "never" do something. Suggesting so is likely to provoke a defensive rather than accepting response.

Deliberately try to use "and" rather than "but" or "however" when you move from a cushioning, positive feedback statement to a developmental one. For example, you could say, "Bob, you are a very effective employee, but there is the issue of coming late to work." Or you could say, "Bob, you are a very effective employee, and then there is the issue of coming late to work." Subtly but importantly, the second version is easier for listeners to receive. "And" gives little offense, while contrast words like "but" are provocative, automatically raising listeners' defenses and reducing their ability to both listen and think clearly.

In a behavioral feedback session, also pay attention to staying in the present. Negative behaviors ignored six months ago should not be surfaced now. If a behavior deserves feedback then give that feedback within forty-eight hours of when it occurred. Otherwise, forget it.

Finally, rather than *telling* individuals what to do in response to feedback, ask them what *they* think they should do about it. If they come up with an action, they are also more likely to buy into it and own it. The general frame of mind should be new commitment rather than submission to orders from above. Once the junior leader sees a workable solution, then the two of you can move on to goals for the process, developing an action plan that achieves desired behavioral change.

Performance Appraisals

Count on leaders to pay close attention to all assessed behaviors on which their merit increase, bonus, and promotion possibilities are based! In other words, performance appraisals and their related reviews and evaluations are great venues for behavioral feedback regarding character development. The appraisal context reinforces a leader's perceptions of how positive and influential their best leadership behaviors are, and it will motivate them to look for further positive adjustments.

The important goal here is to leverage behavioral assessments inherent to the performance appraisal process. Intuitively and as a matter of professional survival, leaders will emphasize and do those things they are held accountable for and on which they will be evaluated. They will also avoid those things they should not do if they know that negative consequences will fall on them. This "gain and pain model" makes use of a natural and normal response. Leaders will do what is to their advantage (gain) and will avoid what works against them (pain). Placing behavioral objectives in the cadre's performance appraisals raises the probability that future behaviors will be positive.

For example, look at how the attribute of communication lends itself to leader performance appraisals. Suppose that sharing information is an objective in the performance appraisal, and suppose a cadre member purposely does not share information. Further suppose that in between annual appraisals, at quarterly and other occasional feedback sessions, you've pointed out the pattern but still not seen any change. Perhaps you recognize an underlying reason—that possessing exclusive information feels like a form of power. Regardless of the motivation, you will issue a mediocre rating on the annual appraisal in the area of communication, which affects both the merit pay increase and the annual bonus. This is a wake-up call about the consequences of the behavioral choice. At this point, most likely, the junior leader will consciously work on changing the behavior, seeing a clear future benefit in sharing information.

Including behavioral objectives and feedback in a performance appraisal is beneficial also when the cadre member is already doing well in some respect. Another cadre member might have a particular strength in communication and sharing information. The resulting performance review includes an outstanding rating in this area. Pride in that outstanding mark will most likely inspire the recipient to continue this behavior and actually try to improve it so the rating on the next performance appraisal will be outstanding once again.

As these two examples suggest, the appraisal process can be an effective vehicle for character development, promoting and encouraging behaviors that have a positive impact for leadership and in general among employees. The key is to include the relevant behavioral objectives.

Format Options for Performance Appraisals

A human resources department generally develops the performance appraisal forms for its organization based on its vision, values, and standards. Almost all provide some framework for measuring and evaluating behavior. Checklists (often including ratings scales) are common. So are forms based on management by objectives.

As mentioned earlier, for leadership character development, a checklist can be organized around five behavioral attributes—courage, caring, optimism, self-control, and communication (see Appendix C). Relevant behaviors can be rated on a scale or evaluated in written comments. Checklist ratings can also include traditional character-related words or phrases such as integrity, ethical conduct, personal morality code, strong value base, and so on. As a retired army officer, I am very familiar with evaluation as a leadership development tool. The U.S. Army follows an excellent model for developing leadership character through the performance appraisal process. It has been placing items relating to character on performance appraisals for years. Few organizations match the extensive character evaluation of a leader found in the army's current officer's efficiency report, DA Form 67-9. Part IV of that two-page evaluation (one-quarter of the total report) is titled "Character." In it are ratings on all seven of the army's organizational values: honor, integrity, courage, loyalty, respect, selfless service, and duty. In it also are ratings on leader attributes, skills, and actions (behaviors). A subheading "Influencing" covers communicating, decision making, and motivating. An officer who receives less than a top score on this rating will probably have poor prospects for promotion.

On the army's current noncommissioned officer efficiency report (NCO-ER) there is a rating for "integrity," which embraces doing what is legally and morally right, possessing high personal moral standards, and being honest in word and deed. Performance is rated as excellent, successful, or needing improvement (Walker, 2005).

Performance appraisals of educational institutions also offer interesting models in that they routinely place equal emphasis on leadership attributes and performance results. For example, the University of California, Berkeley, has an entire section evaluating the leader's communication skills (available on its Web site). These include written expression, oral expression, willingness to share information, tact, and diplomacy. Behaviors are rated on a scale from "outstanding" to "unacceptable."

The performance appraisal for professional staff at Case Western Reserve University (Case Western's Performance Management Outline) lists communications performance competencies under the heading *Attention to Communications*. Items include

- Ensures clear, timely communications to others (both oral and written), particularly those who will be affected by the change
- Listens to others carefully and attentively
- Builds effective formal and informal communication channels

Similarly, a University of California performance appraisal from the university president's office also provides for rating communication behavior with a five-point scale for items such as these:

- Clarity of ideas expressed
- Effectiveness of oral and written presentations
- Skill in listening and interacting with others in a helpful manner

(Incidentally, the statement of purpose on the form wisely includes this language: "Informal performance evaluation is the on-going feedback required for effective supervisor/employee relations. The written evaluation should not replace continuing feedback and communications on the job.")

Besides communication, university appraisals implicitly address other leader attributes. For example, a Princeton University staff performance form also includes a rating scale on interpersonal relations that corresponds to caring. It evaluates the extent to which the employee is cooperative, considerate, and tactful in dealing with others. The performance appraisal report of the University of California, Davis, includes individual ratings on communication skills, steadiness under pressure (self-control), developing others (caring), and a combined category of leadership and integrity.

Moving on from general checklists, management by objectives (MBO) sets up behavioral objectives in measurable, quantifiable terms. The Center for Creative Leadership's MBO approach has proven very effective in assessing leadership behaviors. It covers behavioral improvement based on feedback, and feedback on other related behavioral leadership traits, skills, or qualities. Optionally, MBO can have other requirements, such as absence of reported incidents of ethical compromise during the period being rated.

MBO should clarify how a cadre member's behavior is or needs to be made consistent with the organization's vision, values, and current objectives. Many organizations require that both the leader's performance and behavioral objectives support at least one of the organization's stated goals.

Besides checklists and MBO, there are other effective performance appraisal formats: critical incident ratings and narrative or essay rating schemes. Critical incident rating involves describing the behavior of the cadre member in key incidents, situations, or circumstances during the rating period. The incidents or situations are considered representative of the behavior of that individual during the rating period. In the narrative or essay rating format the evaluator writes about the behavioral strengths or developmental needs of the cadre member in a variety of areas, which can include the five attributes, other behaviors, or traditional character themes such as integrity, ethics, values, morals, and so on.

Best Practices in Performance Appraisals

In any annual performance review process, certain best practices can enhance your cadre's leadership positive behaviors. The first is simply that you, the leader, must carefully plan and execute the review and evaluation process. This may sound obvious, but because of job and time pressures, many leaders do evaluations at the last minute. This is unfair to the person being evaluated and sets a weak example of caring.

The job descriptions of junior leaders are extremely important to the process. They should be very specific, clearly listing all behavioral expectations on which the incumbent will be assessed. Providing a thorough job description fits a broader principle of never surprising someone with unannounced expectations. Similarly, do not surprise anyone with assessment information that has not been discussed in detail at relevant times in the course of the period being rated. This is particularly true for character-related information that could have a negative impact on a leader's career. You may know from personal experience how counterproductive this can be. I had an experience with a boss who, in my annual performance evaluation, wrote three statements that could be interpreted as being less than positive. He had never discussed any of these issues with me, and two of the statements were inaccurate. I supplied a rebuttal to the report, and when I discussed the situation with my human resources manager, she said, "Oh yes, your rater is notorious for writing that kind of a report." Apparently others shared my lack of appreciation of this type of treatment.

Also, performance evaluations are not the proper forum for cute or otherwise unprofessional comments about a leader or anyone else. Nonetheless, such comments do appear. Here are several statements that showed up on federal employee performance reviews (Rinkworks, n.d.):

"He would argue with a signpost."

"When she opens her mouth, it seems that this is only to change feet."

"This young lady has delusions of adequacy."

"He certainly takes a long time to make his pointless."

Ideally, a performance appraisal includes input from people besides the rater who know the ratee well. This provides additional insights from people who may have observed situations and behaviors when the rater wasn't present, or who saw things from a different perspective, or who may simply not have the same interests or agenda as a single rater has.

Cadre members should never be asked to write their own evaluation. You, the leader, should have the courage to officially determine and record in the formal appraisal that a member of your leadership cadre has negative, inconsistent, or low-impact behaviors. That your judgment may be controversial or potentially lead to negative fallout is not a reason to avoid recording developmental needs. A leader needs to have the courage to give tough feedback on behaviors when tough is warranted. Not to do this also shows lack of caring for both the ratee and the organization. A free pass on developmental feedback is unfair to the ratee because it encourages inconsistent, negative behaviors to continue. When leaders are silent on a certain behavior, the silence is interpreted by all as approval. If there is a legal issue on your mind when you consider withholding accurate feedback, it's time to consult with your organization's human resources and legal experts. They can help you and your cadre ensure the legality of all performance review behavioral items related to character.

Most often, the presence of character-related behavioral ratings in the formal performance appraisal is enough to motivate your leadership cadre to behave consistently with your organization's expectations, especially when they clearly match your own. Members of one's cadre of leaders who are consistently involved in questionable behaviors do have a habit of ultimately eliminating themselves from the organization.

Finally, because some mediocre managers do exhibit all of the bad habits I've discussed, it bears mentioning that the performance appraisal should not only be completely accurate, it should also be completed on time—not ignored or postponed until long after the organization's deadline. Also, the report should be presented in person and not left on the recipient's desk.

Discipline

The primary function of discipline is to teach cadre members that certain behavior is unacceptable and must be changed if they wish to remain in the organization. How you as leader handle matters of discipline is indicative of your courage, caring, professional competence, and attitudes toward developing others. How you discipline will set the standard for every leader who works for you.

To discipline means to teach, not to carry out justice or punish. When things have reached a state calling for punishment, the right move is to terminate employment. Discipline needs to include instruction to stop a wrong behavior, along with instruction that helps the person take a different, appropriate path. Discipline must include informing someone why they need to change behaviors.

The first or second time, the exchange may be verbal, as part of the ongoing behavioral feedback process discussed earlier in the chapter. Escalated stages of feedback continue to include verbal warnings, but can move from recording the same warning in the individual's personnel file to writing a letter of reprimand or counseling to suspension without pay, and finally to termination. Some people are not teachable; ideally, you would never have hired them in the first place—but if you (or your predecessors) erred in the hiring decision, it is your job to deal with the resulting situation.

If—after coaching, training, sufficient time for a person to change, and support from both you and the organization—a serious negative behavior persists, then termination is best for all involved. A number of leaders have told me that the epiphany of their life came when they got fired. It caused them to reflect and evaluate their behaviors and resolve to change enough so that they'd never repeat the same mistakes. It was a "come to the mountain" experience that changed their lives for the better.

The so-called "10-80-10 rule" applies directly to the discipline process. Of your cadre of leaders or employees, 10 percent will make positive adjustments to their behavior from just your glance or a simple word. They want to know what they are not doing right and will actually respect you highly for caring enough about them to correct them. They have the potential to become your best people. An opposite 10 percent will never make adjustments despite harsh and continuous discipline. Your job as a leader of character is to get that 80 percent in the middle on board and moving in the right direction.

Jack Welch had a standing policy while at General Electric to get rid of the bottom 10 percent of performers every year. This approach of course had a downside: it created much turmoil. However, on the positive side it also accomplished a major cleansing of nonperformers and difficult employees. It is a cleansing process that those who lead sincerely appreciate. It is an option in deciding what to do with that most recalcitrant 10 percent.

But even perennially recalcitrant employees can be disciplined successfully. One of my most memorable experiences at administering discipline involved the administrative assistant I inherited when I was assigned to the U.S. Military Delegation at NATO headquarters in Brussels. This assistant was over seventy years old and had worked for the U.S. government for more than fifty years. When I arrived she said, "Colonel, I view you as summer help. I was here when you got here and I will be here when you leave." With that attitude she had intimidated more than one of my predecessors. However, when I gave her a letter of counseling for continually coming

back late from lunch several things happened. First her performance improved in all areas—probably because no one in fifty years
had ever formally counseled her. Her dislike for me increased significantly. And my stock went up 100 percent in the U.S. Military
Delegation because I had addressed a behavioral situation that had
gone uncorrected not only with my secretary but with many other
secretaries within the delegation. Of course, on bosses' day I did not
get a lot of flowers from my own or the other secretaries. And when
I left NATO two years later my administrative assistant was still
there as she said she would be.

There is an impression among leaders that to care about and
nurture their cadre of leaders and employees is to be overly tolerant,
softhearted, compassionate, and weak. Being sympathetic is also
equated with "running a country club" at work and letting employees do their own thing, never criticizing them, and not holding
them accountable for doing the job. That is as far from the truth as
possible. *To nurture* means simply to do those things that are in the
best professional interests of the individual in both the short and
long term. That includes discipline when it is warranted.

Leaders of character will care about their cadre of leaders and
employees enough to discipline them as necessary. Not to discipline
is not to care. It can even be a sign of extreme dislike or contempt
of one's employees. To skillfully correct another person is one of the
best ways a leader of character can show interest in the individual's
development and future. Employees who are not corrected when it
is called for have the highest potential to cause shame and embarrassment for their leaders and the organization.

Just as many leaders hesitate to give feedback, many leaders hesitate to discipline either their leadership cadre or their employees.
Either they do not discipline their direct reports, or they pass off the
entire responsibility and process to human resources. As with giving feedback, behind their hesitation usually lies one or more of the
following:

- Lack of skill at or knowledge of the discipline process

- Fear of litigation
- Lack of courage to confront
- Discomfort with the potential of conflict
- Fear of possibly making a bad personnel situation even worse

If these are problems for you as a leader, I urge you to overcome them rapidly through some developmental work of your own. Whatever fear, hesitation, or weakness you show during the discipline process will be picked up immediately by the person being disciplined, and this will only make the situation more uncomfortable and tense.

Best Practices in Discipline

Discipline should always be fair, prompt, and focused on maintaining the dignity of the employee. It is always wise to have a third party present, particularly someone from human resources—and of the same gender as the recipient of the discipline if the recipient's gender is different from yours.

Never apologize for the meeting or appear hesitant. Maintain positive self-control at all times and do not become angry or display nonverbal anger. Avoid using sarcasm, flip comments, and, as was discussed earlier, inflammatory words like *always* or *never*.

Be as specific as possible about the behavior in question and why it was inappropriate.

Solicit the recipient's point of view, but watch out for attempts to sidetrack the discussion on unrelated issues or to shift the blame.

Explain your expectations for how the behavior will change, offer your help and support, clearly define the time frame in which the change is expected, and establish a day for a follow-on session that will look for progress. Finally, make sure to clearly understand (by hearing it in the recipient's own words) what the recipient will be doing to change the undesirable behavior.

Every organization has its own procedures for the various levels of the disciplinary process. As a leader of influence, you should know these procedures and be comfortable implementing them. That is the behavior that is expected of you. Regardless of procedures, do not lose sight of the idea that the single purpose of a disciplinary process is to teach the correct and appropriate behavior.

Other Uses of Evaluation in the Character Development Process

With some creative thinking and resourcefulness, you may be able to find or create other evaluation processes in your organization that can be used in the character development process for your leadership cadre. You could include measures like these:

Administering assessment instruments to your leadership cadre that would review their value system, compare and contrast it with the value system of the organization, give insights on how they make choices, outline the process used to determine the consequences of their choices, and so on. These formal instruments could include 360-degree behavioral assessments with evaluations from boss, peers, direct reports, and others. Using 360-degree assessments almost always brings feedback surprises. These surprises are items of behavioral feedback that the feedback giver did not have the courage to offer face to face but could give in a 360-degree format. This can especially be the case when the behaviors involve issues of character and values.

Hire coaches for your leadership cadre who are experts in coaching issues of character. The coach can give your cadre insights and assessments on their behaviors and how to adjust them to be more consistent and positively influential.

The evaluation process can also be used to determine the behavioral impact you and your leadership cadre members have on your employees through indirect morale measurements that take note of such things as incidents of sexual harassment, affirmative action violations, absenteeism, tardiness, sick leave, turnover, complaints, grievances, substance abuse, waste, sabotage, and overall productivity.

You and your cadre can also evaluate yourselves regarding behavioral change and progress through reflection and introspection. You can structure a look at how you choose behaviors, your value system, and your ethical base by answering a series of questions. Questions such as the following can also help you evaluate whether you all currently possess the right motivation, mind-set, and tools to support character development.

- How am I currently doing in my character development process? Am I being consistent in applying behaviors that have a positive influence on others? (Identify specific recent behaviors.)

- In what behavioral areas am I making the most progress in my character development? The least progress?

- What actions am I taking to ensure my own success?

- What things am I *not* doing or what behaviors am I *not* working on whose absence might derail my career?

- How open am I to receiving and acting on behavioral feedback? (Examine some specific situations and the responses you made.)

- In what areas are my behaviors most consistent and influential in a positive way? In what areas are they least consistent or least positively influential?

- What can I do to refine how I make choices and decisions?

- What can I do to more fully understand the consequences of the choices and decisions I make? (Think also about secondary and tertiary consequences.)

Building Leadership Character: Evaluation

1. What do you think of the following statement? "Morals cannot be legislated but behavior can be."

2. How pertinent is evaluation to your current personal leadership style? How evident is it within your current organizational culture?

3. What has been your experience so far using evaluation to develop positive leadership behaviors?

4. How do your current practices in giving behavioral feedback compare with the best-practice suggestions in this chapter?

5. What leadership behavioral objectives are currently part of performance appraisals at your organization? What improvements could be made? (Consider all five leadership attributes.)

6. How might you make discipline a more effective tool for teaching?

Chapter Eight

Next Steps

This brief final chapter frames a general procedure for starting a leadership character development process in your organization. Within this framework you can draw on the numerous activities described in the preceding chapters. The procedure has three basic parts: assessment, planning, and execution and adjustment.

Initiating a development process for leadership character can be personally motivating, even fun. However, it is also a serious challenge and is likely to meet some opposition, both at the outset and further on. Because of this consideration, some of the following may sound somewhat negative. It's not. It's just reminding you to be aware of the challenges so that you can act realistically and with full conviction.

Some members of your cadre may push back and oppose your initiative. They may see it as unnecessary, as a threat, as a waste of valuable time, or as someone else's means to impose a standard of morality on them. They may say nothing at first, but passive-aggressively oppose the program once it begins. You may also have colleagues or superiors who approve a development process but are inwardly very skeptical of its value and outcomes. These are possibilities you as the leader must consider as you go through the assessment, planning, and execution phases of the process. With anticipation, solid communication, a caring attitude, and courageous optimism, resistance can be overcome. But it should be planned for up front.

Before further discussing next steps, however, I'd like to share my own favorite example of what leadership character can do and how it can be achieved. Theodore Roosevelt, the twenty-sixth president of the United States, was both a product of the Five E's and a leader of strength in *all five leadership attributes*. "Teddy" was known as a man of extraordinary courage, iron self-control, and undying optimism. After both his wife and mother died on the same day in 1884, the grieving twenty-six-year-old Roosevelt moved from New York to a ranch in North Dakota. There he would learn lessons from experience that would be the foundation of his successful political life. The Harvard-educated Roosevelt said that working closely with people from all social classes took the snob out of him and helped him connect with people from many different walks of life. It made him more authentic, genuine, and caring. Later, as a New York City police commissioner, he was famous for patrolling with the police in order to learn about what was really happening in the city. The behaviors he developed and exhibited in that environment and culture further helped him identify with the common man and vaulted him into political prominence.

His exemplary courage bridged many phases of his life. For example, he was awarded the Congressional Medal of Honor for his bravery in the Spanish American War of 1898. In 1912, while campaigning for the presidency, he was shot in the chest at point-blank range by an assassin. The bullet went through his folded-over fifty-page speech and also his eyeglasses. It penetrated three inches into his chest but hit no vital organs. Against the advice of his aides, Roosevelt, a master communicator, presented the entire ninety-minute speech before going to the hospital for treatment. Such a pattern of behavior is one of the many reasons his likeness was carved into Mount Rushmore and his legacy and influence are still very strong almost a century later.

Assessment

First, determine your own level of commitment and preparedness to initiate, implement, and follow through with a development process for leadership character.

- What leadership attributes and skills do you have to make this development process effective and successful? Especially assess yourself regarding the five basic attributes presented in detail in Chapter Two (courage, caring, optimism, self-control, and communication).

- Do you currently have enough credibility with your leadership cadre to make those who are tentative and skeptical give the process a chance?

- Will you be able to implement and follow through on your plans for a sustained amount of time, that is, eighteen to twenty-four months? Are you willing to accept the potential criticism and notoriety that may come as a result of your advocating for the value of "character"?

- Do you have the patience, perseverance, and persistence to drive this development process regardless of obstacles you may encounter? What obstacles should you anticipate?

The Readiness of Your Cadre of Leaders

Second, assess the needs of your cadre of leaders, as well as their potential openness to a development process for leadership character. Here are some questions to answer:

- Will they be individually motivated to engage in the process?
- Will they willingly commit the necessary time, effort, and honest emotion?
- Will they think such a process is relevant and valuable?
- Will they actually apply and put into practice the information they receive throughout the process? Will they be able to connect with the process emotionally so as to be able to own and internalize both the process and the information?
- Will they be able to see the relationship between leadership character and their own behaviors?

- What factors might make some of them tend to reject the process out of hand? (For example, will some feel threatened by exposure of previous behaviors or feel unable to measure up to new behavioral standards? Will some feel threatened because the process implies that behaviors can be bad, negative, or destructive?)

- Will some cadre members claim they do not need to be involved because their leadership behaviors are already fine?

- For your leadership cadre, is the best approach likely to be somewhat piecemeal and low-key, or is it likely to be a full-blown initiative?

- Who and how many of your cadre members are likely to not commit themselves to this development process? Who may be hesitant, passive-aggressive, or openly resistant, or may try to undermine the process? Who, by personality and temperament, may not want to be involved because they prefer to be left alone to simply do their job?

- Will some members of the leadership cadre be anxious about receiving feedback regarding the impact and consistency of their leadership behaviors?

- Will some find learning and developing new behaviors overly frustrating, risky, or painful?

- May there be tension among the leadership cadre because some think the development process is not aggressive enough and does not go far enough?

- Will some of them think you aim to impose your own standard of right and wrong behaviors on them?

- May some resort to litigation in order to prevent this initiative?

Give careful thought to how extensive each of these potential problems may be, and how you might defuse them.

Readiness of Your Organization

Third, assess your organizational culture. What aspects of the culture will either support or hold back the process?

- What strengths or weaknesses of the organization's culture may promote or hinder an initiative to develop leadership character? At minimum, consider the current organizational climate and situation, the credibility of its leadership, the morale and attitudes of the workforce, and the political culture.

- In view of the culture and climate, what basic starting point or approach is likely to be most effective? (For example, it may be one or another of the Five E's, rather than all at once.) How can the results of the process be measured? Can they be measured in some tangible way? How will you determine the return on investment and cost-benefit ratio?

- Will the notion of developing leadership character be viewed as being impossible, too difficult, too idealistic, too time-consuming, too sensitive, or even too controversial?

- May a development initiative for leadership character at your workplace be seen as unrealistic because of a perception that character development should take place in the family, in school, in religious institutions, or elsewhere? Is this seen as something that should actually be done in the workplace?

- Will the initiative be a tough sell or viewed as impossible because of the general belief that a person's character is fixed in childhood and that behavioral change for adults is extremely difficult, if not impossible?

- May this process be seen as a waste of time, effort, resources, and emotions—a diversion from the real focus of the company's vision and mission?

- May it be seen as being too controversial or sensitive because it may involve judging what is behaviorally right and wrong, good and bad, fair and unfair, just and unjust?

- In addition to the five leadership attributes explored in this book, what other attributes are relevant to and should be emphasized in your environment and culture?
- Has the organization recently experienced a scandal or a character meltdown of one of its leaders? (If so, it may be very open to a development initiative for leadership character.)

Planning and Coordination

After these assessments, begin your planning by reviewing the Integrated Plan for Developing Leadership Character found in Appendix E. As you work out the plan, review what you are already doing in each of the areas of the Five E's, and consider how effective you currently are in each. What can you build on in each area? What more can be done? Start from your strengths. Which of the five afford the best chances of high behavioral impact and positive change?

Planning in the Five E's

As part of planning, be sure to review also what other leaders and organizations have done to develop leadership character.

Example. Review the example you are setting in each main attribute. What other exemplary figures (past and present) can you call on in your process?

Experience. You may already have moved members of your leadership cadre from one job to another specifically to broaden their experience. If so, you can make more use of it. Plan to ensure all the members of your cadre get the variety of experiences needed to develop their leadership behaviors both now and in the future. This will require working closely with human resources, your leadership peers, and more senior leaders in the organization.

Education.   Here also there is a good chance that you already provide some training related to character, ethics, and integrity. If so, you can take it still further. If not, informal discussions with your cadre about constructive behavior can be a way to start exploring the power of education.

Keep in mind that while training can be effective, it's not a panacea. Don't let other leaders who know its current popularity as a solution try to turn it into a behavioral cure-all. This trend is all too obvious on the Web sites of numerous Fortune 500 companies. Unfortunately, the general feedback regarding classes and programs is that they are boring, unrealistic, too idealistic, and a general waste of time overall. But if you focus on discussing ethical dilemmas and reinforcing your organization's ethical philosophy, it will not be difficult for you to surpass what's been going on in other places.

Environment.   Again, consider the makeup and personality of your leadership cadre, the culture of your organization, and the current business situation in which you are operating. Also look for models.

Here are two organizations that have developed cultures of positive leadership behavior: the Synovus Financial Corporation and the Center for Creative Leadership. The Synovus Financial Corporation is routinely ranked among the hundred best companies to work for in the United States. Its CEO, James Blanchard, has institutionalized a culture that emphasizes ethical values, trust, respectful and dignified treatment of employees, and the highest possible standards of customer service. The reason Blanchard has been so successful in this process is that he moves leaders out of the organization if they do not live up to its cultural and behavioral standards (Maxwell, 2003b).

At the Center for Creative Leadership (CCL), everything done in its day-to-day activities as well as the information in its training programs is focused on leadership development and implicitly on the development of leadership character. The result is a positive culture that values its employees, promotes high morale, instills pride, and causes its employees to want to come to work.

Evaluation. You may already include objectives related to leadership character on performance evaluations. If so, they might offer another starting point. An old adage says that morality cannot be legislated. That is so, but *behavior* can certainly be affected by legislation. You can create and reshape behavioral guidelines and standards that your cadre will comply with to promote their own best interests, regardless of any other feelings.

Very likely you are already doing many of these things. If so, you have a foundation on which to build.

Coordination

I mentioned earlier that broadening your leaders' experience requires coordination with other parts of the organization, including human resources. This is just one aspect of coordinating planning for leadership development.

Since your leadership cadre will be the program's focus, discuss the development initiative with them before it gets under way. Communicate about it in detail so they will understand what it is and what it isn't. Point out the positives and be prepared to allay concerns about possible negatives. You will already know what they are from your assessment process.

These discussions can take place in a series of sessions. The first would be simply an information session, to outline why you are considering such an initiative, its goals, and what it may consist of or look like. You may ask for initial impressions and reactions. Provide an outline of the process and allow future participants some time to think about it before the next meeting. At that meeting you can get their input on what the program should or shouldn't look like and their thoughts on how to proceed. This process of involving your leadership cadre in the planning will strengthen their buy-in and ownership. It will also help you differentiate those members of your cadre who are already 100 percent on board from others who need more convincing. Make clear to all in your cadre of leaders that once the development process is implemented, the amount of support given to it will be rewarded and also reflected on the individual cadre members' annual performance appraisals.

From those on board, assign or ask for a volunteer to be your project leader for the initiative. Optimally, this person will already rate well in terms of courage, optimism, caring, communication, and self-control. You are still the champion of the initiative, but now it also becomes a professional development opportunity for the project leader.

This will probably be the time to determine what resources are required, starting with budget considerations. How much of this year's budget or next year's can go to this development initiative? How large is your leadership cadre? What do you need by way of supporting materials of all types, facilities, audiovisual equipment, information technology (IT) equipment and support, trainer costs, travel and lodging, and the other hidden costs that always seem to crop up? One very important resource is simply actual stories regarding human behavior that will make discussions and workshops meaningful, interesting, entertaining, and even amusing. A good story goes a long way toward making a development process interesting and enjoyable.

Besides coordinating with your cadre and for resources, talk to your boss about what you are thinking of doing. Be prepared to convey a significant level of detail regarding budget, time, and personnel impact. You will need to have a solid argument for how the program can achieve a worthwhile cost-benefit ratio. This involves comparing the cost of an ongoing character development program with the financial impact of the negative publicity and other costs that attend a leadership character lapse. Litigation costs alone from a breach of leadership character may actually be twenty times the cost of a robust development program, or even greater.

You may also want to meet with your organization's training department to brief them about your emerging plans. It is worthwhile to get their impressions and to find out if they have done or are planning to do anything in the area of leadership development that could augment your program. Also find out what support they can provide—trainers, facilitators, training rooms, materials development, audiovisual support, and so on.

A meeting with your IT department may also be in order to see about automated support. This could include laptop computers, assessment or survey assistance, programming, and so on.

As the leader of the initiative you should do much of this initial coordination yourself, with training, IT, and others, to ensure their correct understanding of the project and the emphasis you are placing on it. Further coordination can be delegated to a project leader you appoint. Have that person accompany you at most initial meetings so that the hand-off will be smooth.

Execution and Adjustments

Once you begin to implement this development process, you will need to monitor all aspects of it—all Five E's—and address problems as soon as possible. Your most likely problem is concerns from your leadership cadre regarding the effectiveness of the process and the time it is consuming. Problems regarding logistics, format, and other details obviously also require attention.

Keep detailed notes on all aspects of the process so that you can make adjustments the next time you repeat an activity. Also hold after action reviews (AARs) periodically with the leadership cadre, at least after every formal training session.

About a year after starting, you can review the entire development process to determine what has been effective and what has not, the tangible results, and the return on investment. At that point you will be able to determine whether the process should continue and in what form.

Your Legacy as a Leader

As we progress in years we begin to think about things that we would not have given the first consideration when we were younger. Introspectively, we ask ourselves, "What difference does my life make? What will its meaning be? Am I fulfilling my ultimate purpose and destiny? What will have to have happened in the next few years for me to say I lived the life I wanted to live?" In short: "What's my legacy now, and what do I want it to be?"

Recently, the board of directors of a major corporation removed its CEO because he was having a consensual affair with a female executive. This CEO was in his sixties and most likely had behind him a record of impressive achievement. Too bad he's likely to be remembered mostly for why he had to leave.

When people leave organizational life, their former colleagues generally remember them by a single sentence. When a name comes up, it does so in the form of a one-sentence legacy: "Chris was a really hard worker." "I wonder if Sally is getting to work on time at her new company." "George was certainly a good guy; I wish he was still here."

Think about what you want your own one-sentence legacy to be. Jim Smith, a CCL adjunct faculty member, urges us to strive to "finish well." Among other things he means finishing our careers with very sound and strong character, with a reputation for consistent, positive, influential behavior. One comedian put it this way: when we were born we were crying and everyone else was happy; when we die we should be happy and everyone else should be crying. That is finishing well.

Stephen Covey (1991) says we can each determine our legacy from here on by starting it right. Decide what you want to be or have achieved by the end, then work back to now and establish a plan that will get you there. How do you want to be remembered at the end of your life? What do you want people to say about your character, pattern of behavior, impact, and overall influence? Try answering that question by writing your own one-sentence character legacy. Then where do you need to start? With perspective and understanding of their past and current behaviors, leaders can adjust those behaviors for greater positive influence and higher overall impact.

Leadership character is all about choosing a behavior—words or deeds—and then accepting the consequences of that behavior. When all is said and done, choices really make the person. That is the essence of leadership character. As animal activist Jane Goodall said, "You cannot get through a single day without having an impact on the world around you. What you do makes a difference, and you have to decide what kind of difference you want to make" (Munier, 2004).

Building Leadership Character: Next Steps

1. Why are planning and assessment important to the final success of a development process for leadership character?

2. What in your experience could you apply to a leadership character development process that would ensure its effectiveness and success?

3. How would you go about initiating a development process for leadership character within your current organizational environment?

4. Now that you have this information, what will you do with it?

Personal Values

Have you ever asked yourself what is important to you? What things do you value? On what do you base your choices? Fundamentally all your choices, decisions, and other leadership behaviors are driven by and based on your personal value system. This is true of everyone. Everything we choose to do is a reflection of our personal value system. This includes our habits, how we talk, how and what we eat, our work ethic, who we have as friends and who we hang around with, our hobbies, how we spend our time, the movies we see, the books we read, how we spend our money, how we vacation, our spiritual life, and the quality of our relationships. Gloria Steinem said that we can tell our values by looking at our checkbook stubs (Munier, 2004). Ralph Waldo Emerson called people's actions only a picture book of their personal "creed," by which he meant values. A working adult's value system fundamentally consists of five areas: self, vocation (career), relationships, community, and spirituality.

This self-assessment will assist you in identifying and clarifying your personal value system. Before you begin, think of yourself reading the entire story of your life. What has been really important to you? What has really mattered to you? What has lasting value to you? What do you really not want to lose or give up? What are some things you really love? Be as honest as possible. Then perform these steps in order:

1. Briefly review the following lists and circle those items in each area that you value. Use the blank lines to add any items that you feel are missing.

2. Rank the top five items in each list with one being the item most valued.

3. Look at the twenty-five items you ranked and come up with the top five things you value.

The results will increase your self-awareness and may surprise you.

Values Related to Self:

Academic accomplishment and degrees	Appearance and image	A school
Education and intellectual growth	Physical fitness	A team
Knowledge	Recognition	Clothes
Achieving goals	Self-respect and esteem	House
Activity and action	Responsibility	Property
Affiliation and belonging	Wisdom	Attention
Courage	Social status	Approval
Decisiveness	Addictions	Sex
Affluence and economic security	Doing something well	Skills
Wealth	Athletic prowess	Vacations
Self-indulgence	Physical health	Memories
Balance	Emotional health	Car or cars
Hobbies and collections	Material possessions	Time
Creativity	Television programs	Gardening
Enjoyment	Movies and DVDs	Admiration
Music and singing	Golf or fishing	Love
Happiness and joy	Integrity	Fame
Humor and laughing	Reading	Writing
Influence and impact	Legacy	Speaking
Political party	A dream, goal, or vision	Researching
Self-actualization	Fulfillment	An idea
Personal development	Contentment	Dancing
_____	_____	_____

Vocational Values:

Achieving goals	Activity	Balance
Promotion	Authority	Challenge

Affiliation and belonging	Collaboration	Duty
Autonomy and independence	Vision and goal	Dream
Change and variety	Competence	Courage
Achieving results	Creativity	Expertise
Compensation	Productivity	Trust
Family-like environment	Justice	Location
Diverse perspectives	Loyalty	Recognition
Variety of skills	Rewards	Status
Influence and impact	Self-respect and esteem	Responsibility
Developing others	Symbols of success	An idea or ideas
Doing something well	Time	Bonuses
An organization	Job security	Respect
Dignified treatment	Opportunities	Advancement
Position	Title	Office
Profits	ROI	Perks
_____	_____	_____

Relationship Values:

Family	Friends	Fellowship
Camaraderie	Love	Support
Bonding	Sense of community	Loyalty
Diversity and perspectives	Developing others	Sex
Respect	Dignified treatment	Goodwill
Sharing children's lives	Cooperation	Harmony
_____	_____	_____

Community Values:

Helping others	Sense of community	Justice
Location	Duty	A cause
Neighborhood	An organization	Volunteering
Altruism	Humanitarianism	Diversity
Service	Contributing time, money, resources	Publicity
_____	_____	_____

Spiritual Values:

God	Tolerance	Respect
Religion	Balance	Integrity
Honesty	Morality	Ethics
Aesthetics	Meditation	Reflection
Introspection	Retreats	Moderation
Wisdom	Duty	Responsibility
Contentment	Fulfillment	Inner peace
Optimism	Forgiveness	Love
Hope	Faith	Heaven
An organization	A place	A facility
_____	_____	_____

Appendix B

Assessing Leadership Character

Choices, options, and trade-offs all involve many considerations. Asking character-related questions can help to clarify and sort out difficult decisions. Consider the following:

1. Am I looking at the situation correctly? Are emotional inhibitors causing me to read the situation inaccurately?

2. What are the alternative courses of action? What are the good and bad consequences of each?

3. What is really the "right" and mature thing to do?

4. Which choices are consistent with my organization's value system? With my value system?

5. Are organizational values conflicting with my own as I weigh this decision? If so, how can I resolve that?

6. Are any of the choices illegal, unethical, or dishonorable?

7. Is what I am about to say or do straightforward? Am I misrepresenting anything, attempting to deceive, or giving disinformation?

8. Is the truth being compromised in any way by my decision or actions?

9. If my true motives for choosing the way I did came to light, could it cost me major embarrassment or even my job?

10. What would the leader I respect most or my mentor do in this situation? What would my boss do?

11. If someone I respected asked me for advice in a similar situation, what advice would I give?

12. What would my mom, dad, or grandparents say about my choice?

13. Could this choice cause my boss, family, friends, or organization embarrassment?

14. Could this choice cause a subordinate to report my actions to my boss or human resources?

15. Could this choice cause someone to report my actions to the news media? Would I say and do the same thing if the *60 Minutes* news team were standing here taping?

16. Will I eventually need a lawyer because of this decision? Do I have the resources (time, money, resolve) for extended litigation?

17. Will I have to be looking over my shoulder for the rest of my career as a result of the choice I am about to make?

18. What does the "voice of conscience" tell me I should do?

19. Will I be able to live with myself, considering the consequences of the choice I am about to make?

20. Would I have to go to confession because of this choice?

21. Did I avoid the truth in answering any of these questions?

A Checklist of Good Leader Behaviors

Courage

Shows Vision

☐ Thinks in terms of an uncertain future.

☐ Often shares ideas about meeting the future.

☐ Addresses difficult job requirements.

☐ Takes on broader and more difficult problems and issues.

☐ Creates and initiates significant organizational change.

Accepts Risk and Responsibility

☐ Faces problems in spite of fear.

☐ Evaluates risks.

☐ Takes appropriate risks on promising, unproven methods.

☐ Takes personal as well as business risks.

☐ Has the fortitude to be a whole person at work.

Acts

☐ Looks at issues in terms of actions.

☐ Acts when others hesitate or delay.

☐ Acts to expedite the decisions of others.

☐ Acts even in the face of opposition.

☐ Demonstrates good conscious inaction (not jumping too quickly).

Decides

- ☐ Is not paralyzed or overwhelmed by a need to decide.
- ☐ Makes effective and timely decisions.
- ☐ Does not procrastinate on controversial or potentially divisive decisions.
- ☐ Weighs potential consequences.
- ☐ Does not overthink a decision.
- ☐ Does not continually seek more information to delay a decision.
- ☐ Does not allow decisions to take shape by indecision or default.
- ☐ Does not rush decisions to get them over with.
- ☐ Enjoys troubleshooting and solving problems.
- ☐ Follows through as soon as a decision is made.
- ☐ Moves forward toward goals despite chaos.

Delegates and Manages

- ☐ Cultivates decision-making skills in others.
- ☐ Delegates meaningful responsibilities to capable others.
- ☐ Assigns appropriate tasks and decisions to the team.
- ☐ Delegates at the appropriate time.
- ☐ Stays in touch with others about delegated work.
- ☐ Advocates for the team and protects it from inappropriate internal and external interference.
- ☐ Holds teams and individuals accountable for outcomes.
- ☐ Ensures that others are recognized and rewarded for their contributions.
- ☐ Deals directly with difficult people.
- ☐ Does not shy away from evaluating the work of others.
- ☐ Does not shy away from counseling, disciplining, or dismissing employees.

Perseveres

☐ Does not get discouraged easily.

☐ Addresses all responsibilities including unpleasant or disagreeable ones.

☐ Perseveres in the face of problems and difficulties.

☐ Persists in the face of criticism.

☐ Does not compromise when convinced of something.

☐ Persists at securing needed resources.

Addresses Conflict

☐ Recognizes and acknowledges conflict.

☐ Confronts conflict promptly to prevent escalation.

☐ Does not shy away from conflicts with juniors.

☐ Takes the lead on unpopular though necessary actions.

☐ Is skilled at presenting contrary opinions.

☐ Is able and willing to confront others as needed.

☐ Pursues feedback even when others are reluctant to give it.

☐ Takes positions that may seem unpopular or politically incorrect.

☐ Stands up to the boss in defense of strong evidence or belief.

☐ Remains effective when tensions run high.

Shows Independence and Resourcefulness

☐ Thinks independently for the overall good.

☐ Steps back to see that actions and decisions make broad sense.

☐ Honestly evaluates ongoing progress.

☐ Comes up with novel ideas and improvements.

☐ Uses resources creatively and efficiently.

☐ Strives to be as competent and professionally effective as possible.

☐ Gathers knowledge needed to reduce uncertainty and fear.

Stays Self-Aware and Self-Sustaining

☐ Has positive, courageous role models.

☐ Spends time with those who lend encouragement.

☐ Is not afraid to ask others about the impact of his or her own challenging actions.

☐ Seeks feedback and actually changes as a result.

☐ Acknowledges own personal feelings in situations of change.

☐ Makes effective use of mental or spiritual practice.

Caring

Practices Good Basic Social Skills

☐ Is competent at dealing with people's feelings.

☐ Has a disposition and personality that puts people at ease.

☐ Does not annoy or antagonize people.

☐ Has a good and appropriate sense of humor.

☐ Is able to apologize and ask for forgiveness.

Hears Others

☐ Is readily available to others.

☐ Makes time to listen.

☐ Acknowledges the limits of own point of view.

☐ Gathers others' perspectives.

☐ Can view a situation through others' eyes.

☐ Seeks to learn from others' experiences.

Nurtures and Develops Others

☐ Nurtures others' ambitions.

☐ Shows interest in others' needs, hopes, and dreams.

☐ Helps others connect with their passions and their work.

☐ Allows new people in a job sufficient time to learn.

☐ Helps people learn from their mistakes.

☐ Provides employees with challenge and opportunity.

☐ Coaches employees in how to meet expectations.

☐ Interacts with staff in a way that adds to their motivation.

☐ Helps employees with personal problems as needed.

☐ Is sensitive to signs of overwork in others.

Recognizes and Uses the Talents of Others

☐ Recognizes, appreciates, and uses the strengths of others.

☐ Willingly delegates prestigious and enjoyable tasks, not just un-appealing, unglamorous ones.

☐ Involves key people in planning and new action.

☐ Rewards hard work and dedication to excellence.

☐ Actively promotes direct reports to senior management.

Regards People Fairly and Individually

☐ Relates positively and cooperatively with superiors, direct reports, peers, and outsiders.

☐ Values different backgrounds and perspectives.

☐ Treats everyone fairly.

☐ Treats people as individuals.

☐ Does not play favorites.

☐ Makes good use of people and does not exploit them.

Works Well with People of Different Backgrounds

☐ Understands and respects cultural, religious, gender, and racial differences.

☐ Finds value in differences.

☐ Is skilled at relating to, getting along with, and working with different types of people.

☐ Is comfortable managing people from different racial or cultural backgrounds.

☐ Works to improve such skills.

☐ Makes personnel decisions based on appropriate factors.

Monitors Personal Effect on Others and on Groups

☐ Studies how own personality and needs affect team performance.

☐ Stays aware of own personal feelings and biases.

☐ Is open to feedback regarding own behavior toward others.

Deals Well with Others in Times of Change

☐ Manages own emotions and feelings in situations of change.

☐ Looks out for others in times of change.

☐ Takes into account people's concerns and feelings when initiating change.

☐ Manages others' resistance to organizational change.

☐ Welcomes and respects honest expression of feelings in reaction to change.

☐ Shares own feelings appropriately in times of change.

☐ Helps others learn how to handle stress.

Optimism

Shows a Positive Attitude and Commitment

☐ Is optimistic.

☐ Displays a positive and cheerful attitude.

☐ Is upbeat, energetic, and can-do.

☐ Insists that most problems can be solved.

☐ Stays committed to success.

Challenges Negative Formulations and Assumptions

☐ Critically examines problem definitions as first stated.

☐ Looks for better ways to define a problem.

☐ Always assumes a problem has more than one right answer.

Looks for Possibilities

☐ Accepts change as positive and necessary for growth and progress.

☐ Looks for opportunity hidden in negative situations.

☐ Sees multiple positive possibilities.

☐ Finds ways to experiment.

☐ Has an experience-based belief in the notion of serendipity.

☐ Tolerates ambiguity well.

☐ Constantly offers novel ideas and perspectives.

☐ Does not lapse into routine and sameness.

☐ Pushes the organization.

Inspires Optimism

☐ Creates a productive atmosphere for others.

☐ Fosters a climate of experimentation.

☐ Transmits optimism and excitement to others.

☐ Sets a contagious example.

☐ Leads by example and "walks the talk."

☐ Sets a pace that others will follow.

☐ Approaches teamwork with a positive attitude.

☐ Methodically builds supports for actions.

Responds Well to Setbacks

☐ Does not deny setbacks.

☐ Views setbacks as opportunity for learning.

☐ Bounces back quickly and honestly from failure.

☐ Finds ways to help others bounce back.

Stays Tuned to the Future

☐ Sees the value of ongoing best practices.

☐ Supports activities that position the organization for the future.

☐ Most often correctly judges which creative ideas will pay off.

Shows Self-Acceptance

☐ Stays aware of own accomplishments.

☐ Does not deny or hide mistakes.

☐ Is willing to admit not knowing.

☐ Is self-aware and comfortable with self.

Self-Control

Shows Long-Term Patience and Endurance

☐ Shows patience and endurance for completing projects.

☐ Holds self accountable.

☐ Takes charge in troubled times.

☐ Does not commit prematurely.

Adapts

☐ Tolerates ambiguity and uncertainty.

☐ Suspends judgment until needed information is available.

☐ Adapts readily to new situations.

☐ Welcomes rather than complains about change.

Maintains and Projects Personal Calm

☐ Stays calm, confident, and steady in difficult moments and times.

☐ Is consistent in behavior whether things are going well or not.

☐ Stays focused when others are confused.

☐ Stays on task.

Coordinates Well with Others

☐ Clearly conveys objectives, deadlines, and expectations.

☐ Knows when to intervene and when to stand by.

☐ Is involved where and when needed.

☐ Accepts need to depend on others beyond own control.

☐ Gives employees control when they are ready.

☐ Gradually increases employees' responsibilities as appropriate.

☐ Allows talented people to do their jobs without interference.

☐ Allows others to learn from honest mistakes.

Handles Own Emotions Well

☐ Is aware of own feelings and need to control them.

☐ Is aware of how personal biases affect own attitude and outlook.

☐ Stays composed under pressure.

☐ Does not get angry even when a situation may warrant it.

☐ Does not become hostile or moody when things are not going well.

☐ Does not blame others or claim to be a victim.

☐ Does not shift responsibility.

☐ Controls emotions related to feedback.

Uses Own Strengths Well

☐ Knows and capitalizes on own strengths.

☐ Knows and compensates for own weaknesses.

☐ Responds well to new situations that require stretch or growth.

Stays in Control of Self

☐ Controls own career, not expecting others to plan it.

☐ Handles mistakes and setbacks with professional poise.

☐ Responds to greater autonomy by working hard to develop professional skills.

Deals Well with Personal Stress

☐ Balances life in a way that allows maintaining emotional equilibrium.

☐ Anticipates and prepares for stressful situations.

☐ Has the personal support system for coping with emotional overload.

☐ Avoids agitating others with own tension and anxiety.

☐ Keeps stressors in perspective and does not dwell on them.

☐ Uses constructive outlets for tension and frustrations.

Controls Appetites and Exercises

☐ Eats right.

☐ Avoids misuse of alcohol and drugs.

☐ Maintains appropriate sexual boundaries.

☐ Does not overindulge in gambling or other risky pursuits.

☐ Exercises regularly.

☐ Keeps in touch with medical help.

Communication

Speaks Well

☐ Speaks crisply, clearly, and articulately.

- ☐ Expresses ideas fluently and eloquently.
- ☐ Commands attention and respect.
- ☐ Inspires enthusiasm.
- ☐ Presents logical and compelling arguments.
- ☐ Articulates complex concepts well.
- ☐ Advocates well for what he or she believes is right.
- ☐ Uses stories, metaphors, examples, and images to share ideas.
- ☐ Often gives encouragement and reassurance.

Performs Well

- ☐ Prepares for role in any gathering.
- ☐ Speaks well in public.
- ☐ Performs well on stage.
- ☐ Has the skill to entertain.
- ☐ Is able to inspire and motivate groups.
- ☐ Is able to persuade.
- ☐ Handles resistant audiences well.
- ☐ Negotiates well.

Writes Well

- ☐ Organizes ideas well on paper.
- ☐ Communicates appealingly in writing.
- ☐ Writes clearly and concisely.
- ☐ Seeks writing assistance as needed.
- ☐ Documents problems and progress.
- ☐ Keeps up essential correspondence.

Communicates Well Nonverbally

- ☐ Understands symbolic value of personal visibility daily and on special occasions.

☐ Assesses impact of own nonverbal communication on others.

☐ Projects confidence, poise, and respect.

☐ Expresses acceptance and encouragement through gesture.

☐ Ensures that own nonverbal and verbal messages are aligned.

Communicates the Positive Vision of the Organization

☐ Often communicates the organization's vision.

☐ Paints a clear, attractive picture of the organization's future.

☐ Conveys confidence and steadiness during difficult times.

☐ Clarifies specific goals and plans.

Listens Actively and Well

☐ Notices when others want to speak.

☐ Listens to individuals from all levels of the organization.

☐ Stops to listen.

☐ Asks questions or paraphrases others to clarify meanings.

☐ Solicits employee views both when things are going well and when they are not.

☐ Listens carefully to others' ideas and suggestions.

☐ Lets people know they have been truly heard.

Practices and Encourages Open Communication

☐ Encourages direct and open discussion.

☐ Initiates difficult but needed conversations.

☐ Is clear about expectations.

☐ Influences others by means other than formal authority.

☐ Disseminates information quickly and clearly.

☐ Provides timely, ongoing positive and negative feedback.

☐ Keeps others informed of future changes that may affect their work or environment.

☐ Stays open to constructive feedback.

☐ Shares information.

Strengthens Team Communication

☐ Plans meetings.

☐ Runs meetings efficiently.

☐ Creates good give-and-take with others in group conversations.

☐ Appropriately delegates meeting tasks such as note-taking, timekeeping, and so on.

☐ Asks good questions.

☐ Solicits information and opinions from others.

☐ Seeks input from all team members.

☐ Involves others before developing a plan of action.

☐ Addresses concerns and gains commitment before implementing changes.

Stays Aware of Multicultural Differences

☐ Actively studies relevant global or regional differences and commonalities.

☐ Keeps own cultural viewpoints in check when interacting with a person from another culture.

☐ Communicates well with others who differ by gender, ethnic background, or nationality.

☐ Tailors communication to others' perspectives, motivations, and agendas.

Keeps Higher-Ups Informed

☐ Finds out what superiors want without waiting for instructions.

☐ Keeps higher-ups and peers informed.

☐ Communicates anticipations rather than delivering late and unpleasant surprises.

☐ Is skilled at selling upward, influencing superiors.

Appendix D

Leadership Character Scenarios

Use the following short situations for thought and discussion. All are leadership scenarios involving choices, responses, and consequences. For each, a good starting point is to ask the group how a leader with strong positive leadership behaviors and character might handle the situation. Then ask how it might be handled by a leader with weaker character resources. In each case, ask group members to explain the reasoning behind their remarks.

Scenario #1. James, one of your key subordinates and a solid performer, has recently become heavily involved in coaching his son's Little League baseball team. Your boss just now informs you that your company's major Japanese client is coming unexpectedly in three days and that your department will have to make a major presentation. Preparation will require you and your whole staff to work late for the next two nights. You share this with James, who responds by telling you that he will be involved in Little League playoff games both tomorrow night and the following night and therefore cannot stay late. He tells you that his assistant Jean can stay late and provide the input you need. How do you respond?

Scenario #2. You have just received a transfer and a promotion to operations manager of the most successful plant in your corporation. Since you are only thirty-two-years old, this is an extraordinary achievement. When you arrive at your new job, the current plant manager (who is also your new boss) gives you a tour of the plant and proceeds to introduce you to the employees. When he introduces you to your main direct report, Al, you extend your hand and say, "It's a pleasure to meet you. I've heard many good things about you." Al, who is fifty-four-years old, neither acknowledges your hand nor looks at you but says, "I'm planning to retire." Then he turns and starts to walk away. Several of your other new direct reports are watching this situation unfold. How will you respond?

Scenario #3. You make a suggestion to your boss regarding a novel solution to a problem that has plagued your company for the past three years. Your boss seems uninterested and says he will give your suggestion some thought when he has more time. A month goes by and you hear nothing about the suggestion. Then you see an announcement that your boss will be getting a $10,000 suggestion award at a company ceremony on Friday. As you continue to read the flyer you realize that the suggestion for which your boss is getting the award is in fact your suggestion. What will you do?

Scenario #4. Homer, who is on your staff and who is a real problem employee, tells you he is considering leaving the company. The next day you receive a phone call from an organization where Homer has interviewed and given your name as a reference. The caller asks what kind of a performer Homer is. You really want to get rid of this guy. What will you say on this phone call?

Scenario #5. You have just been promoted to a new position and have inherited an administrative assistant with it. You notice that on each of your first five days, your assistant departs for lunch at the same time and returns from lunch anywhere from ten to twenty minutes late. What, if anything, will be your response?

Scenario #6. In a one-on-one meeting with your boss (who is a senior vice president in the company), she emphatically tells you to take a certain controversial action on a project. You do as she has instructed, and you think nothing more about it. Later you find out the company president was livid about what you did and confronted your boss. Your boss told the president she didn't know that you had taken this action and that you were operating on your own initiative. What will you do?

Scenario #7. Six months ago you hired Bruno to be your new sales department manager. Very flamboyant, loud, and outgoing, Bruno was put in charge of your seven salespeople, all of whom are young, aggressive, and impressionable. You hired Bruno because he had a track record of "getting the sales!" After six months of having him on the job, sales have increased about 5 percent, which is not as much as you had hoped. Meanwhile, the disturbing trend is that sales staff are now dressing less conservatively, are becoming loud, have started using coarse language, and have begun to tell potentially offensive jokes. Furthermore, their expense reports seem to be getting larger and larger. Since they are representing you in the field, what actions, if any, will you take?

Scenario #8. You, your wife, and two of your key direct reports go out to dinner with a prospective client. Your boss wants very much to do business with this client and tells you to "bend over backwards" to take care of him. The prospective client has a number of alcoholic drinks. He then becomes loud and profane, and starts telling what you consider inappropriate stories. Everyone in the restaurant is now focused on your table and your intoxicated client. How will you handle the situation?

Scenario #9. At the annual strategic planning meeting, you make a key presentation to a group of fifty people that includes the chief executive officer and president of the company. After you present some vital statistics that you have personally verified and know to be correct, one of your peers, with whom you have an ongoing rivalry, challenges your statistics and essentially implies to the entire group that you don't know what you are talking about. This brings a hush to the room. All eyes turns to you for a response. What will you say or do?

Scenario #10. You are responsible for nine project managers who have daily contact with all your major customers. The customer with whom you do the most business telephones you and requests that Dick Jones, the project leader you regard as having the highest potential, be taken off her project immediately. The reasons she gives are rather vague and nebulous. This takes you completely by surprise. What will you do?

Scenario #11. You are in charge of eighteen administrative personnel. One month ago you hired an attractive young computer operator who is bright, hardworking, and a quick study. She asks to speak to you privately and at that meeting alleges that one of the male employees, someone who has worked for you for ten years, has on at least three occasions made sexual advances toward her. This seems to be out of character for that male employee, who is quiet and very reliable overall. The computer operator asks you to ensure there are no further occurrences of these advances or she will have no alternative but to file a formal sexual harassment complaint. What will you do?

Scenario #12. You have a minority employee who has been counseled on seven occasions over the past three years regarding substandard performance. All of the counseling has stemmed from customer complaints that were investigated and found to be valid. This employee has openly stated that legal action will be initiated against the company if he is ever terminated. Additional training and coaching has not resulted in any noticeable improvement in the employee's performance. Last week still another valid customer complaint was received. (Your company has previously come under unfounded criticism in the local news media for alleged discriminatory practices.) What will you do regarding this latest complaint?

Scenario #13. You are chief of the contracting and purchasing department of an organization that is about to ask for bids for a mega construction project. You are called by a senior official of a large construction company that is very interested in taking on this project. The caller tells you that if you provide them with certain inside information that will help his company land this multimillion-dollar contract, he will give you $2.5 million in a Cayman bank account. What will you do?

Scenario #14. A certain component that your organization manufactures is required by federal law to meet a certain safety standard. In the course of your daily activities you become aware of the real possibility that in order to meet a customer deadline, one of your peers has approved the release of a large number of these components that do not meet this safety standard. What will you do?

Scenario #15. You direct your employee, Bobbie, to use the Minnesota State method for the project on which she is working. As a result of this method, the project fails and your company loses a large sum of money. When your boss asks why Bobbie failed so miserably and suggests she be demoted and transferred to a less responsible position, what will you say?

Scenario #16. You are at a meeting with fifty of your organization's senior leaders and managers. The new CEO has just outlined a new corporate strategy. In doing so he says that greater profits, higher margins, and substantial cost cutting are the order of the day. Since personnel costs are the company's greatest expenditure, the CEO indicates that this is where everyone is to begin. He adds that the notion of taking care of your employees is a bunch of bunk. This organization, he adds, is not a social service or a day care center. If the employees don't like how they are being treated they can leave. They aren't chained to their desks or their machines. After he finishes saying this, he looks around the room and his eyes make contact with yours. He then asks you, "What are your impressions of our new strategy?" What will you say?

Scenario #17.   An army unit captures two slightly wounded enemy soldiers after a brief firefight. Shortly thereafter, the unit gets orders to move to a new position. The platoon leader knows the prisoners need to be escorted to the rear for interrogation, treatment of their wounds, and P.O.W. processing. Prior to moving out he tells one of his young sergeants to take care of the prisoners. He then hears two shots. He looks and sees that the sergeant has just shot both prisoners. Outraged, the platoon leader, yells, "Why did you do that?" The sergeant replies, "Well, you told me to take care of the prisoners." Evaluate the communication process between the platoon leader and the sergeant.

Integrated Plan for Developing Leadership Character

1. *Purpose:*

   In this section, state the purpose of the plan. The essence of it will be to provide a guideline for an organizational process to develop leadership character.

2. *Definitions:*

   In this section, define terms, especially those about which there may be some confusion or misunderstanding. Here are examples:

   - *Leadership character:* behaviors that have a positive influence on others.
   - *Character development:* the expansion of an individual's ability to be consistent in a pattern of positive, influential behaviors.

3. *Assumptions:*

   In this section, state important assumptions to avoid misunderstanding. Supplement this list as necessary.

   - Character can be further adjusted and developed in adults.
   - Continuous learning is essential to both leadership development and character development.

- It is both realistic and practical to implement a development process for leadership character within a public, private, or nonprofit organization.
- Because of the emphasis, example, creativity, and resources required, the leaders of the organization are the key to the success of the entire process.
- The aim of a leadership character development process is preventive and therefore the time and resources allocated are to be viewed as an investment and not a waste or an abuse of assets.
- The development process for leadership character is not in any way aimed at promoting any moral, spiritual, or religious agenda.

4. *Responsibilities:*

   This section should include a listing of the responsibilities of the organization's leaders at various levels, human resources, and the training department. It should also indicate who will be the lead individual, any project managers or assistants, and who is held accountable for specific areas of the process.

5. *Resources to be allocated to the character development process:*

   In this section, list funds, facilities, time allocation, materials, and internal and external personnel—trainers, consultants, coaches, and your organization's leaders—to be used in the character development process. Consider also listing specific learning resources available for the process—for example, training; courses; and educational center materials such as books, CDs, DVDs, or online opportunities.

6. *Time lines:*

   Establish the time schedule and all significant process deadlines.

7. *The Framework of the Five E's:*

> The Five E's will be the framework for developing charac-ter by example, experience, evaluation, education, and environment.

- *Example:* In this section, at minimum include focus on the following positive behavioral examples: courage, caring, optimism, self-control, and communication.
- *Experience:* Focus on internal professional development opportunities that would enhance the development of leadership character.
- *Evaluation:* Include receiving and applying behavioral feedback, the performance appraisal process, and the or-ganization's employee discipline philosophy.
- *Education:* At minimum, include the training approach and means to develop positive leadership behaviors.
- *Environment:* Include gaining an understanding of the or-ganization's value system and, from that information, de-termining what patterns of behavior are compatible with your organizational culture.

8. *Measurements of success of the leadership character development process:*

> In this section, indicate expected outcomes of the process, such as the following:

- No ethical violations or abuses.
- No organizational scandals.
- No resources expended on negative character behaviors.
- No complaints from customers, clients, and suppliers about behavioral lapses on the part of the organization's personnel.
- A more harmonious and professional operating culture based on fewer grievances, formal complaints, or instances of interpersonal conflict.

- An assessment of the depth and clarity of understanding, the level of engagement, and general buy-in. (These conclusions will be based on surveying and individually questioning those involved in the development process.)
- Solicited and unsolicited feedback from the cadre members and other employees regarding the impact of the program.

9. *Rewards and recognition:*

In this section, specify rewards for those who support the process and contribute significantly to its overall success.

10. *Other:*

References and Suggested Readings

Adenauer, K. (1965–1968). *Konrad Adenauer, Erinnerungen* [reminiscences] *1945–1963* (vols. 1–4). Stuttgart, Germany: Deutsche Verlags-Anstalt.

Adrian, L. (Ed.). (2001). *The most important thing I know: Life lessons from Colin Powell, Stephen Covey, Maya Angelou and 75 other eminent intellectuals.* Kansas City: Andrews McMeel.

Anderson, E. (Ed.). (1981). *Thoughts for our times.* Cleveland, OH: Pilgrim Press.

Anderson, P. (Ed.). (1992). *Great quotes from great leaders.* Lombard, IL: Successories.

Armstrong, L. (2000). *It's not about the bike.* New York: Putnam.

Axelrod, A. (2003). *Profiles in leadership: The distinctive lives of men and women who shaped history.* Upper Saddle River, NJ: Prentice Hall.

Baldwin, D., & Grayson, C. (2004). *Influence: Gaining commitment, getting results.* Greensboro, NC: Center for Creative Leadership.

Barber, J. D. (1992). *The presidential character: Predicting performance in the White House.* Upper Saddle River, NJ: Prentice Hall.

Barnett, R. (2003). *Winning without losing your way: Character-centered leadership.* Bowling Green, KY: Winning Your Way.

Bennett, W. (Ed.). (1993). *The book of virtues.* New York: Simon & Schuster.

Bennett, W. (2001). *Virtues of leadership.* Nashville, TN: Thomas Nelson.

Borba, M. (2002). *Building moral intelligence: The seven essential virtues that teach kids to do the right thing.* New York: Wiley.

Brands, H. W. (2002). *The first American: The life and times of Benjamin Franklin.* New York: Anchor Books.

Bredeson, C. (1996). *Presidential Medal of Freedom winners.* Springfield, NJ: Enslow.

Bridges, W. (1980). *Transitions: Making sense of life's changes.* Philadelphia: Perseus Books.

Brophy, B. (2005, October 31). Thomas L. Friedman, columnist: The journalist as globalist. In *U.S. News & World Report*, Special Report/Special Issue: America's Best Leaders, pp. 38–40.

Bundles, A. (2001). *On her own ground: The life and times of Madam C. J. Walker.* Princeton, NJ: Scribner.

Buron, R. J., & McDonald-Mann, D. (1999). *Giving feedback to subordinates.* Greensboro, NC: Center for Creative Leadership.

Calarco, A., & Bader, P. (2003, January/February). Adaptability: What it takes to be a quick change artist. *Leadership in Action, 22*(6), 3–6.

Callahan, D. (2004). *The cheating culture: Why more Americans are cheating to get ahead.* Orlando, FL: Harcourt.

Campbell, D. P., & Nilsen, D. (1998). *Campbell Leadership Index development planning guide.* Minneapolis, MN: NCS Pearson.

Cawthorne, N. (2005). *Tyrants: History's 100 most evil despots and dictators.* New York: Barnes & Noble.

Chandler, D. B. (1973). *The campaigns of Napoleon.* Princeton, NJ: Scribner.

Clark, K. (2005, October 31). Donna Shalala, president, University of Miami: A whirlwind's winning ways. In *U.S. News & World Report*, Special Report/Special Issue: America's Best Leaders, pp. 30–32.

Coles, R. (2000). *Lives of moral leadership.* New York: Random House.

Collins, J. (2001). *Good to great.* New York: Harper Business.

Conflict Dynamics Profile technical guide. (2001). St. Petersburg, FL: Eckerd College Management Development Institute.

Cooper, T. L., & Wright, D. (1992). *Exemplary public administrators: Character and leadership in government.* San Francisco: Jossey-Bass.

Copeland, M. V. (2005, December). My golden rule: 30 leaders share their secrets to success, *Business 2.0.* Available online: http://money.cnn.com/magazines/business2/business2_archive/2005/12/01/toc.html. Access date: May 15, 2006.

Covey, S. (1991). *Principle-centered leadership.* New York: Fireside.

Cox, H. (2004). *When Jesus came to Harvard: Making moral choices today.* Boston: Houghton Mifflin.

Crocker, H. W. (1999). *Robert E. Lee on leadership: Executive lessons in character, courage and vision.* New York: Crown.

Degregario, W. (1997). *The complete book of U.S. presidents.* New York: Gramercy.

Department of the Army, Office of the Chief of Military History. (1947, March 15). *The command decision* (MS No. 080A). Washington DC: U.S. Government Printing Office.

DeRoche, E. F., & Williams, M. H. (2000). *Educating hearts and minds: A comprehensive character education framework.* Thousand Oaks, CA: Sage.

Di Frances, J. (2002). *Reclaiming the ethical high ground: Developing organizations of character.* Wales, WI: Reliance Books.

Doh, J., & Stumpf, S. (Eds.). (2004). *Handbook on responsible leadership and governance in global business.* Philadelphia: University of Villanova Press.

Dotlich, D. L., & Cairo, P. C. (2003). *Why CEOs fail: The 11 behaviors that can derail your climb to the top—and how to manage them.* San Francisco: Jossey-Bass.

Douglas, C. (2003). *Key events and lessons for managers in a diverse workforce: A report on research and findings.* Greensboro, NC: Center for Creative Leadership.

Drucker, P. F. (1967). *The effective executive.* New York: HarperCollins.

Drucker, P. F. (2004, June). What makes an effective executive? *Harvard Business Review, 82*(6).

Duffy, B. (2005, October 31). Colin Powell, soldier, statesman: The kid of no promise. In *U.S. News & World Report,* Special Report/Special Issue: America's Best Leaders, p. 36.

Elder, L. (1998, July 3). Stereotyping Al Campanis. *FrontPageMagazine.com.* Available online: www.frontpagemag.com/Articles/Printable.asp? ID=2886. Access date: June 26, 2006.

Emerson, R. W. (1876). *Letters and social aims.* Boston: Osgood.

Fernandez, J. (2005, March 2). Putting character in the curriculum. (Greensboro, NC) *News and Record,* p. A1.

Fleming, J. (2003). *Profit at any cost? Why business ethics makes sense.* Grand Rapids, MI: Baker Books.

Fleming, P. (1999). *The long program: Skating toward life's victories.* New York: Pocket Books.

Ford, G. R. (1979). *A time to heal: The autobiography of Gerald R. Ford.* New York: HarperCollins.

Fulghum, R. (2004). *All I really need to know I learned in kindergarten* (rev. ed.). New York: Ballantine Books.

Gaebelein, T. A., & Simmons, R. P. (2000). *A question of character: Life lessons to learn from military history.* Long Island City, NY: Hatherleigh Press.

Gardner, H. (1983). *Frames of mind: The theory of multiple intelligences.* New York: Basic Books.

Gardner, H., Csikszentmihalyi, M., & Damon, W. (2002). *Good work: When excellence and ethics meet.* New York: Basic Books.

Graham, B. (1997). *Just as I am: The autobiography of Billy Graham.* San Francisco: HarperSanFrancisco.

Greenleaf, R. K. (1998). *The power of servant leadership.* San Francisco: Berrett-Koehler.

Guinness, O. (Ed.). (2000). *Character counts: Leadership qualities in Washington, Wilberforce, Lincoln, Solzhenitsyn.* Grand Rapids, MI: Baker Books.

Guinness, O., & Mooney, V. (Eds.). (2000). *When no one sees: The importance of character in an age of image.* Colorado Springs, CO: NavPress.

Gutierrez, C. M. (2005, December). Believe in something bigger than yourself. In M. V. Copeland, My golden rule: 30 leaders share their secrets to success, *Business 2.0.* Available online: http://money.cnn.com/ magazines/business2/business2_archive/2005/12/01/toc.html. Access date: May 15, 2006.

Haberbosch, V. (2002). *Lessons learned in the desert: Exploring lessons of leadership and character*. Lincoln, NE: iUniverse.

Hamilton, N. A. (1999). *American business leaders: From colonial times to the present*. Santa Barbara, CA: ABC-Clio.

Hargie, O., & Tourish, D. (2004). How are we doing? Measuring and monitoring organizational communication. In O. Hargie & D. Tourish (Eds.), *Key issues in organizational communication*. New York: Routledge.

Harvard Business Review on corporate ethics. (2003). Boston: Harvard Business School Press.

Harvey, J. B. (1996). *The Abilene Paradox and other meditations on management*. San Francisco: Jossey-Bass.

Hayden, T. (2005a, October 31). Bill Drayton, CEO, Ashoka: Entrepreneur for social change. In *U.S. News & World Report*, Special Report/Special Issue: America's Best Leaders, pp. 63–66.

Hayden, T. (2005b, October 31). Roger Ailes, chairman and CEO, Fox Channel: Natural-born networker. In *U.S. News & World Report*, Special Report/Special Issue: America's Best Leaders, pp. 56–58.

Hillman, J. (1999). *The force of character and the lasting life*. New York: Ballantine Books.

Hirschmann, K. (2003). *Leadership (character education)*. Oxford, England: Raintree.

House, R. J., Hanges, P. J., Javidan, M., Dorfman, P. W., & Gupta, V. (Eds.). (2004). *Culture, leadership, and organization: The GLOBE study of 62 societies*. Thousand Oaks, CA: Sage.

Hybels, B. (1987). *Who you are (when no one is looking): Choosing consistency, resisting compromise*. Downers Grove, IL: InterVarsity Press.

International Bible Society. (1978). *Holy Bible: New international version*. Grand Rapids, MI: Zondervan.

Internet encyclopedia of philosophy. (2006). Aristotle (384–322 B.C.E.): General Introduction. Available online: www.utm.edu/research/iep/a/aristotl.htm. Access date: May 15, 2006.

Jeffreys, G., & Heatherly, C. (1992). *Jim Gardner: A question of character*. Raleigh, NC: Patriot Press.

Joicey, C. (Ed.). (2002). *Americans: Paintings and photographs from the National Portrait Gallery*. New York: Watson-Guptill.

Josephson, M. (1959). *Edison: A biography*. New York: McGraw-Hill.

Judge, W. Q. (1999). *The leader's shadow: Exploring and developing character*. London: Sage.

Jung, C. G. (1976). *The portable Jung*. New York: Penguin Books.

Kaplan, R. E. (1990). *Character shifts: The challenge of improving executive performance through personal growth*. Greensboro, NC: Center for Creative Leadership.

Kennedy, D. J. (1994). *Character and destiny: A nation in search of its soul*. Grand Rapids, MI: Zondervan.

Kennedy, J. F. (1956). *Profiles in courage*. New York: HarperCollins.

Kerns, C. (2005). *Value-centered ethics: A proactive system to shape ethical behavior*. Amherst, MA: HRD Press.

Kidder, R. M. (1995). *How good people make tough choices: Resolving the dilemmas of ethical living*. New York: Morrow.

Kirkland, K., & Manoogian, S. (1998). *Ongoing feedback: How to get it, how to use it*. Greensboro, NC: Center for Creative Leadership.

Klann, G. (1999). A model for developing ground combat leaders. Unpublished doctoral dissertation. Free University of Brussels, Belgium.

Klann, G. (2003a). Character study: Strengthening the heart of good leadership. *Leadership in Action, 23*(3), 3–7.

Klann, G. (2003b). *Crisis leadership*. Greensboro, NC: Center for Creative Leadership.

Klann, G. (2004). *Building your team's morale, pride, and spirit*. Greensboro, NC: Center for Creative Leadership.

Knight, P. (2006). *Bowerman and the men of Oregon: The story of Oregon's legendary coach & Nike's co-founder*. New York: Rodale.

Kohlberg, L., & Turiel, E. (1971). Moral development and moral education. In G. Lesser (Ed.), *Psychology and educational practice*. New York: Scott Foresman.

Laborde, G. Z. (1994). *Influencing with integrity*. Mountain View, CA: Syntony.

Lazarus, S. (2005, December). Business can't trump happiness. In M. V. Copeland, My golden rule: 30 leaders share their secrets to success, *Business 2.0*. Available online: http://money.cnn.com/magazines/business2/business2_archive/2005/12/01/toc.html. Access date: May 15, 2006.

Lee, G. (2006). *Courage, the backbone of leadership*. San Francisco: Jossey-Bass.

Leslie, J., & Van Velsor, E. (1995). *A look at derailment today: North America and Europe*. Greensboro, NC: Center for Creative Leadership.

Lickona, T. (1991). *Educating for character: How our schools can teach respect and responsibility*. New York: Bantam Books.

Lickona, T. (2004). *Character matters: How to help our children develop good judgment, integrity, and other essential virtues*. New York: Touchstone.

Lombardo, M., & Eichinger, R. (2004). *FYI For your improvement: A guide for development and coaching* (4th ed.). Minneapolis: Lominger Limited.

Mansfield, S. (2002). *Never give in: The extraordinary character of Winston Churchill*. Nashville, TN: Cumberland House.

Maraniss, D. (1999). *When pride still mattered: A life of Vince Lombardi*. New York: Simon & Schuster.

Marchica, J. (2004). *The accountable organization: Reclaiming integrity, restoring trust*. Palo Alto, CA: Davies-Black.

Marshall, S. L. A. (1989). *The armed forces officer*. Quantico, VA: Marine Corps Association Bookstore.

Maslow, A. H. (1987). *Motivation and personality* (3rd ed.). New York: HarperCollins.

Maxwell, J. C. (1993). *The winning attitude*. Nashville, TN: Nelson.

Maxwell, J. C. (2000). *Failing forward: Turning mistakes into stepping stones for success*. Nashville, TN: Nelson Business.

Maxwell, J. C. (2003a). *Ethics 101*. New York: Center Street.

Maxwell, J. C. (2003b). *There's no such thing as business ethics: There is only one rule for making decisions*. New York: Warner Business Books.

McCain, J. (2005). *Character is destiny*. New York: Random House.

McCall, M., Lombardo, M., & Morrison, A. (1988). *The lessons of experience: How successful executives develop on the job*. New York: Free Press.

McCauley, C., & Van Velsor, E. (Eds.). (2004). *The Center for Creative Leadership handbook of leadership development* (2nd ed.). San Francisco: Jossey-Bass.

McGregor, D. (2005). *The human side of enterprise* (annotated ed.). New York: McGraw-Hill. (Original work published 1960)

McKay, M., & Fanning, P. (2000). *Self-esteem: A proven program of cognitive techniques for assessing, improving, and maintaining your self-esteem*. New York: Barnes and Noble.

Meyers, W. (2005, October 31). Howard Shultz, chairman of Starbucks: Conscience in a cup of coffee. In *U.S. News & World Report*, Special Report/Special Issue: America's Best Leaders, pp. 48–50.

Molesworth, C. (1991). *Marianne Moore: A literary life*. Boston: Northeastern University Press.

Montgomery, B. (1958). *Memoirs of Field Marshal Viscount Montgomery of Alamein*. London: Collins.

Moran, C. M. W. (1987). *Anatomy of courage*. New York: Avery. (Original work published 1945)

Munier, P. (2004). *On being blonde: Wit and wisdom from the world's most infamous blondes*. Gloucester, MA: Fair Winds Press.

Neelman, D. (2005, December). Never, ever forget that you are a servant. In M. V. Copeland, My golden rule: 30 leaders share their secrets to success, *Business 2.0*. Available online: http://money.cnn.com/magazines/business2/business2_archive/2005/12/01/toc.html. Access date: May 15, 2006.

Newmark, C. (2005, December). Choose your mistakes carefully. In M. V. Copeland, My golden rule: 30 leaders share their secrets to success, *Business 2.0*. Available online: http://money.cnn.com/magazines/business2/business2_archive/2005/12/01/toc.html. Access date: May 15, 2006.

O'Mara, P. (1978). *The character of a Christian leader*. Ann Arbor, MI: Servant Books.

O'Neil, W. (2004a). *Business leaders and success: 55 top business leaders and how they achieved greatness*. New York: McGraw-Hill.

O'Neil, W. (2004b). *Sports leaders and success: 55 top sports leaders and how they achieved greatness*. New York: McGraw-Hill.

Paine, L. S. (2002). *Value shift: Why companies must merge social and financial imperatives to achieve superior performance*. New York: McGraw-Hill.

Parsons, D. (2005, December). Whatever a man soweth, that shall he also reap. In M. V. Copeland, My golden rule: 30 leaders share their secrets to success, *Business 2.0*. Available online: http://money.cnn.com/magazines/business2/business2_archive/2005/12/01/toc.html. Access date: May 15, 2006.

Pauchant, T. C. (Ed.). (2002). *Ethics and spirituality at work: Hopes and pitfalls in organizations*. Westport, CT: Quorum Books.

Peters, R. (1999). *Fighting for the future: Will America triumph?* Mechanicsburg, PA: Stackpole Books.

Phillips, D. T., & Loy, J. M. (2003). *Character in action: The U.S. Coast Guard on leadership*. Annapolis, MD: Naval Institute Press.

Piaget, J. (1965). *The moral judgment of the child*. New York: Free Press.

Piper, T., Gentile, M. C., & Parks, S. D. (1993). *Can ethics be taught? Perspectives, challenges, and approaches at the Harvard Business School*. Boston: Harvard Business School Press.

Poll: A leadership deficit. (2005, October 31). *U.S. News & World Report,*p. 80.

Puryear, E. F. (1981). *Stars in flight: A study in Air Force character and leadership*. New York: Ballantine Books.

Puryear, E. F. (2002). *American generalship: Character is everything: The art of command*. Novato, CA: Presidio Press.

Raatma, L. (2002). *Leadership*. Mankato, MN: Capstone Press.

Remick, N. T. (2003). *West Point: Thomas Jefferson: Character leadership education: The cadet four years*. Warren Grove, NJ: RPR.

Rinkworks. (n.d.). Things people said: Employee performance evaluation quotes. Available online: www.rinkworks.com/said/employees.shtml. Access date: May 15, 2006.

Robey, D. (2003). *The power of positive habits*. Miami, FL: Abritt.

Rochelle, B. (1993). *Witness to freedom: Young people who fought for civil rights*. New York: Puffin Books.

Rubenzer, S. J., & Faschingerbauer, T. R. (2004). *Personality, character, and leadership in the White House: Psychologists assess the presidents*. Dulles, VA: Brassey's.

Rudolph, W. (1977). *Wilma*. New York: New American Library.

Sandburg, C. (2002 reprint). *Abraham Lincoln: The prairie years and the war years*. Fort Washington, PA: Harvest Books. (Original work published 1939)

Schultz, S. (2005, October 31). Bill and Melinda Gates, founders, Bill and Melinda Gates Foundation: For a healthier globe. In *U.S. News & World Report*, Special Report/Special Issue: America's Best Leaders.

Schutz, W. (1958). *FIRO: A three dimensional theory of interpersonal behavior*. New York: Holt, Rinehart & Winston.

Schutz, W. C. (1996). *FIRO-B booklet*. Mountain View, CA: Consulting Psychologists Press.

Schwarzkopf, H. N. (1993). *It doesn't take a hero: The autobiography of General H. Norman Schwarzkopf*. New York: Bantam.

Seidenberg, I. (2005, December). Hard work opens doors. In M. V. Copeland, My golden rule: 30 leaders share their secrets to success, *Business 2.0*. Available online: http://money.cnn.com/magazines/business2/ business2_archive/2005/12/01/toc.html. Access date: May 15, 2006.

Seligman, M. E. P. (1998). *Learned optimism: How to change your mind and your life*. New York: Pocket Books.

Senske, K. (2003). *Executive values: A Christian approach to organizational leadership*. Minneapolis, MN: Augsburg Fortress.

Shackleton, E. (1992). *South: The story of Shackleton's last expedition*. North Pomfret, VT: Trafalgar Square. (Original work published 1926)

Sheehy, G. (1988). *Character: America's search for leadership*. New York: Morrow.

Simon, S. B., Howe, L. W., & Kirschenbaum, H. (1995). *Values clarification: A practical, action-directed workbook*. New York: Warner Books.

Singer, P. (1993). *Practical ethics* (2nd ed.). Cambridge, England: Cambridge University Press.

Smith, P. (1997, January). Learning to lead. *Marine Corps Gazette*, pp. 36–40.

Soshnick, S. (2006, January 17). Colts' Manning shows us why he's no Tom Brady. Bloomberg.com. Available online: www.bloomberg.com/ apps/news?pid=10000039&sid=aU1_RApWE8Xg&refer=columnist_ soshnick. Access date: June 26, 2006.

Stogdill, R. M. (1974). *Handbook of leadership: A survey of literature*. New York: Free Press.

Stoufer, S. (Ed.). (1949). *The American soldier: Combat and its aftermath* (vols. 1–5). Princeton, NJ: Princeton University Press.

Terry, R. W. (1993). *Authentic leadership: Courage in action*. San Francisco: Jossey-Bass.

Thompson, M. (2000). *Ethics*. London: NTC.

Thomson, D. (2002). *Scott, Shackleton, and Amundsen: Ambition and tragedy in the Antarctic*. New York: Thunder's Mouth Press.

Thrall, B., McNicol, B., & McElrath, K. (1999). *The ascent of a leader: How ordinary relationships develop extraordinary character*. San Francisco: Jossey-Bass.

Ting, S., & Scisco, P. (Eds.). (2006). *The CCL handbook of coaching: A guide for the leader coach*. San Francisco: Jossey-Bass.

Towers, B. (Ed.). (1996). *The handbook of human resources*. Malden, MA: Blackwell.

Truman, H. S. (1999). *Memoirs of Harry S. Truman: 1945, the year of decisions* (reissued ed.). New York: Konecky. (Original work published 1955)

Tsouras, P. G. (Ed.). (2000). *The Greenhill dictionary of military quotations*. London: Greenhill Books.

Unell, B., & Wyckoff, J. L. (1995). *20 teachable virtues*. New York: Perigee Books.

Vaughn, D. J. (2000). *The pillars of leadership: Foundational character studies of ten great leaders*. Nashville, TN: Cumberland House.

Velasquez, M. G. (1992). *Business ethics, concepts and cases*. Upper Saddle River, NJ: Prentice Hall.

Walker, W. (2005). *The NCO-ER leadership guide*. Manassas Park, VA: Impact.

Warren, R. (2002). *The purpose driven life*. Grand Rapids, MI: Zondervan.

Wasserstrom, R. (1975). *Today's moral problems*. New York: Macmillan.

Weider, B. (n.d.). Chapter 3, Battle of Toulon, September 19, 1793. In International Napoleonic Society, Chronological table of the principal events in the life of Napoleon. Available online: www.napoleonicsociety. com/english/TableOfEvents_page1.htm Access date: May 15, 2006.

White, C. (2005). *Nelson the admiral*. Gloucestershire, UK: Sutton.

Wilkins, A. L. (1989). *Developing corporate character: How to successfully change an organization without destroying it*. San Francisco: Jossey-Bass.

Wooden, J. (1997). *Wooden: A lifetime of observations and reflections on and off the court*. Chicago: Contemporary Books.

Woods, R. L. (1982). *Dilemmas: What would you do if . . . ?* Baltimore, MD: Avalon Hill.

Yukl, G. (1989). *Leadership in organizations*. Upper Saddle River, NJ: Prentice Hall.

Zander, E. (2005, December). At the height of success, "break" your business. In M. V. Copeland, My golden rule: 30 leaders share their secrets to success, *Business 2.0*. Available online: http://money.cnn.com/magazines/ business2/business2_archive/2005/12/01/toc.html. Access date: May 15, 2006.

Zuckerman, M. B. (2004, September 6). Time for a teaching tune-up. *U.S. News & World Report*, p. 94.

Index

About the Center for Creative Leadership

The Center for Creative Leadership (CCL) is a nonprofit, educational institution with international reach. Since the Center's founding in 1970, its mission has been to advance the understanding, practice, and development of leadership for the benefit of society worldwide.

Devoted to leadership education and research, CCL works annually with more than two thousand organizations and twenty thousand individuals from the private, public, education, and nonprofit sectors. The Center's five campuses span three continents: Greensboro, North Carolina; Colorado Springs, Colorado; and San Diego, California, in North America; Brussels, Belgium, in Europe; and Singapore in Asia. In addition, sixteen Network Associates around the world offer selected CCL programs and assessments.

CCL draws strength from its nonprofit status and educational mission, which provide unusual flexibility in a world where quarterly profits often drive thinking and direction. It has the freedom to be objective, wary of short-term trends, and motivated foremost by its mission—hence our substantial and sustained investment in leadership research. Although CCL's work is always grounded in a strong foundation of research, it focuses on achieving a beneficial impact in the real world. Its efforts are geared to be practical and action oriented, helping leaders and their organizations more effectively achieve their goals and vision. The desire to transform learning and ideas into action provides the impetus for CCL's programs, assessments, publications, and services.

Capabilities

CCL's activities encompass leadership education, knowledge generation and dissemination, and building a community centered on leadership. CCL is broadly recognized for excellence in executive education, leadership development, and innovation by sources such as *Business-Week*, the *Financial Times*, the *New York Times*, and the *Wall Street Journal*.

Open-Enrollment Programs

Fourteen open-enrollment courses are designed for leaders at all levels, as well as people responsible for leadership development and training at their organizations. This portfolio offers distinct choices for participants seeking a particular learning environment or type of experience. Some programs are structured specifically around small group activities, discussion, and personal reflection, while others offer hands-on opportunities through business simulations, artistic exploration, team-building exercises, and new-skills practice. Many of these programs offer private one-on-one sessions with a feedback coach.

For a complete listing of programs, visit http://www.ccl.org/programs.

Customized Programs

CCL develops tailored educational solutions for more than one hundred client organizations around the world each year. Through this applied practice, CCL structures and delivers programs focused on specific leadership development needs within the context of defined organizational challenges, including innovation, the merging of cultures, and the development of a broader pool of leaders. The objective is to help organizations develop, within their own cultures, the leadership capacity they need to address challenges as they emerge.

Program details are available online at http://www.ccl.org/custom.

Coaching

CCL's suite of coaching services is designed to help leaders maintain a sustained focus and generate increased momentum toward achieving their goals. These coaching alternatives vary in depth and duration and serve a variety of needs, from helping an executive sort through career and life issues to working with an organization to integrate coaching into its internal development process. Our coaching offerings, which can supplement program attendance or be customized for specific individual or team needs, are based on our ACS model of assessment, challenge, and support.

Learn more about CCL's coaching services at http://www.ccl.org/coaching.

Assessment and Development Resources

CCL pioneered 360-degree feedback and believes that assessment provides a solid foundation for learning, growth, and transformation and that development truly happens when an individual recognizes the need to change. CCL offers a broad selection of assessment tools, online resources, and simulations that can help individuals, teams, and organizations increase their self-awareness, facilitate their own learning, enable their development, and enhance their effectiveness.

CCL's assessments are profiled at http://www.ccl.org/assessments.

Publications

The theoretical foundation for many of our programs, as well as the results of CCL's extensive and often groundbreaking research, can be found in the scores of publications issued by CCL Press and through the Center's alliance with Jossey-Bass, a Wiley imprint. Among these are landmark works, such as *Breaking the Glass Ceiling, The Lessons of Experience*, and *The Center for Creative Leadership Handbook of Leadership Development*, as well as quick-read guidebooks focused on core aspects of leadership. CCL publications provide insights and practical advice to help individuals become more effective leaders, develop leadership training within organizations, address issues of change and diversity, and build the systems and strategies that advance leadership collectively at the institutional level.

A complete listing of CCL publications is available at http://www.ccl.org/publications.

Leadership Community

To ensure that the Center's work remains focused, relevant, and important to the individuals and organizations it serves, CCL maintains a host of networks, councils, and learning and virtual communities that bring together alumni, donors, faculty, practicing leaders, and thought leaders from around the globe. CCL also forges relationships and alliances with individuals, organizations, and associations that share its values and mission. The energy, insights, and support from these relationships help shape and sustain CCL's educational and research practices and provide its clients with an added measure of motivation and inspiration as they continue their lifelong commitment to leadership and learning.

To learn more, visit http://www.ccl.org/connected.

Research

CCL's portfolio of programs, products, and services is built on a solid foundation of behavioral science research. The role of research at CCL is to advance the understanding of leadership and to transform learning into practical tools for participants and clients. CCL's research is the hub of a cycle that transforms knowledge into applications and applications into knowledge, thereby illuminating the way organizations think about and enact leadership and leader development.

Find out more about current research initiatives at http://www.ccl.org/research.

For additional information about CCL, please visit http://www.ccl.org or call Client Services at 336-545-2810.